Parent,
Child, and
Community

Parent, Child, and Community

A Guide for the
Middle-Class
Urban Family

Mack R. Hicks
Herbert Goldstein
Patricia J. Pearson

Nelson-Hall  Chicago

Library of Congress Cataloging in Publication Data

Hicks, Mack R
    Parent, child, and community.

    Bibliography: p.
    Includes index.
    1. Children—Management. 2. Middle classes—United
States. I. Goldstein, Herbert, 1936-   joint author.
II. Pearson, Patricia J., joint author. III. Title.
HQ772.H497   649'.1   79-13816
ISBN 0-88229-231-5

Manufactured in the United States of America

10   9   8   7   6   5   4   3   2   1

This book is dedicated to parents. The authors are convinced that no one, no school, no agency has more understanding of, or love for, a child than the dedicated parent.

The ideas and applications in this book are all drawn from the experiences of parents.

Contents

Acknowledgments

It is impossible to acknowledge each person who assisted the authors in the preparation of this book, but a few names must be mentioned because of their significant contributions.

Our spouses, Susan Hicks and Alene Goldstein, have been very supportive and remarkably patient with us through the years of effort that have gone into this work.

A note of genuine thanks is also due to our children: Philip Hicks, Andrew Hicks, Douglas Hicks, Aimee Goldstein, and David Goldstein. They have all been raised by the book.

Sincere appreciation goes to James B. Raue for artwork, to Philip Hicks for graphics, and to Andrew Hicks for home employment research.

Carol Harrop's secretarial efficiency and organizational skills and Sharon Ingram's excellent typing were major contributions. Ron Yogman's editorial assistance, support, and encouragement were most helpful, indeed, in the final stages of preparing the book.

1 Introduction

This book offers a common-sense, no-nonsense approach to child-rearing—a timely topic, universally in vogue.

The authors have endeavored to cut through the maze of competing and often contradictory theories. The result, we believe, is a well-rounded, better-balanced view of child development and parental involvement.

The authors have also made strong efforts to "tell it like it is."

Most books previously written on the subject have tended to be narrow-minded or distorted in their approach because of a preoccupation with only a part of the whole.

For example, many books represent applications of learning theory (behavior modification) or theories evolving from the "humanistic" school. Many of these books tend to promote a dominant theory or concept and regard the child and his needs, the parents and their needs, the community, genetics, and other factors as less relevant.

Parents who read such books usually develop the notion that most child-rearing problems can be solved through the use of material rewards (behavior modification) or through the group communication and feeling process (humanistic school). These books fail to grapple with the reality that child-rearing is a multidimensional discipline and that simplistic theory and jargon will not suffice. These often misleading approaches exclude a great deal of needed information.

Behavior modification, for example, teaches us *how* to change behavior but not *which* behavior is important to the child's development. The humanistic approach teaches us how to better understand the child's inner feelings and attitudes but not how to recognize his need for external guidelines and his expectations. And neither provides us with information related to the child's specific age.

It is our fond hope that this book brings greater balance and perspective to the field by recognizing the child's individuality and the many community, genetic, and environmental influences that enter the parents' decision-making process. In short, it is the authors' intention that this book take a more realistic and thorough view of the complexities of child development. Our professional credentials have prepared us well for the challenge at hand.

The authors have been engaged in full time independent, private psychologicial counseling practice with child-rearing families for many years. The suggestions and ideas contained in this book, therefore, are not based upon theory but upon practical experience and successful results. The authors are not university professors or theoreticians who may make recommendations based upon a general theory. Rather, the theoretical aspects of this book derive from direct applications and experiences with children and families; theory plays a secondary role.

Too many child-rearing books present a single major philosophy. This is not realistic because of individual differences among children and changes within the same child as he or she progresses over the years. In many cases, first one approach and then another must be tried in order to find the most meaningful and rewarding technique. The question, therefore, is not whether one technique or another is more valuable, but how to apply various child-rearing techniques—and when to call each into play.

The authors' approach is based upon experiences with relatively normal, middle and upper-middle class families. So often in the past, child-rearing books have been written by authors whose experience has been with various socioeconomic levels and various levels of problem behavior—with little or no effort to distinguish these differences.

While applied clinical practitioners have much more "real world" experience than their academic and research-oriented contemporaries, they have the disadvantage of working primarily in clinical settings. There they have been concerned with psychopathology—the exception rather than the norm.

The Developmental Center (the author's home base, which is located in St. Petersburg, Florida), on the other hand, is not a mental health or psychiatric center, and for the most part the families seen at the center represent normal middle-class families who share the same problems and advantages of the authors and readers of this book. It is the authors' objective that this book instruct parents in how to *prevent* and *avoid* problems, rather than how to *solve* problems.

Many child-rearing books have ignored a basic principle of child development. The word "development" itself suggests that children advance through many levels as they grow. Child-rearing principles and techniques should be related to these levels. The four-year-old "runaway" is not to be treated in the same fashion as the sixteen-year-old runaway, for example. Yet many child-rearing books speak of children in general and often recommend the same simplistic approach for children of all ages. It is no wonder that so many parents report they have read many different books and tried "everything" with a child—reasoning, spanking, sending him to his room—only to find that nothing has worked. We know, of course, that no specific technique of child-rearing will work if it is applied at the wrong time, at the wrong age, or at improper intervals.

A major thrust of this book derives from the authors' experience that other factors besides the parent-child relationship are of great significance in the child's development. These include sociological factors beyond the control of the parent, such as the negative influence of the school and other community facilities and agencies, poor architectural design of the home, lack of support from the extended family (grandparents and other relatives), job requirements forcing the family to move from one community to another, various economic crises, poor environmental planning in the community, poor community investment in youth and recreational centers, and too few preventive measures as communities continue to succumb to crisis after crisis and spend more and more money on fewer and fewer children.

In fact, because of the emphasis on community and environment, this book could perhaps be viewed as a sociological text of child development. Prior to the 1960s, parents could count on community factors and influences as relatively steady, unchanging, and reflecting values similar to those taught in the home. As a result, the proper focus of child-rearing was in the relationship between the parent and the child. When parents thought of child-rearing problems and practices, they were concerned mainly with the relationships within the family itself. They could take community and "outside" influences pretty much for granted. Recently, more and more individuals and institutions outside of the family have taken it upon themselves to introduce value systems to the child that they feel are superior to those of the family. They are thus in conflict with traditional values taught within the family.

The authors have also noted a number of children who have developed in a particular way because of maturational lag in the central nervous system, subtle neuropsychological difficulties, genetic predispositions, and early temperamental trait influences. These factors have not been given adequate attention. In addition, many borderline physical problems can make a difference in terms of a child's growth, including vision problems, allergies, coordination difficulties, and hyperactivity.

By recognizing and giving more weight to these other factors, we hope the following will result:

Parents will have greater awareness of these influences and, as a result, take advantage of community resources to build their child's self-confidence while also protecting their child from "family-breakers." In other words, parents will view their community as a sociological maze through which their child must be guided.

Parents will realize that after a certain age is reached they have less influence than the community, peers, and other factors. Parents thus must do their "homework" early to provide a stable base for their children while they are young and while the parents still exert great influence on the child's life.

Parents will no longer feel inadequate because of the problems of one or more of their children even though other children in the family are healthy and well adjusted. Of course, one can argue that the parents are rejecting or scapegoating one child to the benefit of others, and the authors have seen cases in which this is true. In the vast majority of families, in which a child has a behavioral or learning problem, however, we have not found this to be true.

These exceptional cases are best left to the clinical psychologist and other professionals who deal with clinical problems and unusual situations. These difficulties should not be allowed to contaminate norms for child-rearing or influence methods to prevent problems in families.

Because of the lack of awareness of other influences, including genetic and environmental ones, we have seen parents who have made outstanding efforts to raise their children in a proper manner and have followed good, sound child-rearing practices, but who still have children who are mentally ill, delinquent, or drug-abusers. On the other hand, we have seen parents who are poor to mediocre in terms of child-rearing skills but who have children who make solid progress and contribute to their community. These children often have a strong physical and intellectual genetic makeup and have benefited from positive resources in their community.

We have seen many cases in which parents are maligned by "helping agencies" because one or more of their children have problems that, in our opinion, resulted primarily from factors outside of the family.

A popular view is that parents are responsible in a positive or negative direction for 95 percent of their child's personality development. Because of this monumental charge of responsibility, too many parents have become panicked, guilty, and fearful. Consequently, they are too watchful and may "walk on eggs" in their relationships with their children, attempting to understand every nuance of their child's behavior and feelings. In our view, most parents are conscientious and knowledgeable regarding their children, but they need an increased awareness of outside forces that influence their children—and a renewed commitment to the values of the family.

Parents can benefit from guidelines related to what can be expected from a child at certain stages of development as well as gaining a greater awareness of both the positive and negative influences of community and environmental forces. We hope this book will provide parents with these guidelines and this increased awareness.

A final emphasis of this book is the authors' belief that the vast majority of today's youth are not less well adjusted than their predecessors. There are those who would have us believe that the youth of today are weak, self-indulgent, and without merit. Again, we feel these opinions come from individuals who are influenced by the narrow range of children with whom they work. We find these spokesmen to be such people as drug rehabilitation counselors, officials of juvenile courts, mental health workers, and those clergy, police, and school personnel who deal with troubled young people.

Others who share this view come from the groups we term "crisis seekers." These groups receive their income and funding on the basis of crisis, emergency, and alarm. They usually mean well but attempt to make the exception into the rule, often frightening the general public and drawing funding to crisis programs rather than to preventive and developmental programs. Naturally, they are represented as, and quoted as, "experts" on youth. To this extent, these frequently dedicated people are extremely dangerous.

As parents read this book they will see repeated references to children's allowance and income. These figures are based on purchasing power in 1979. They are naturally subject to change with changes in the economy. Parents should be careful, however, to not run ahead of inflation. For example, if our guidelines show that a child is to receive twenty cents for allowance, and it appears that this is too small a figure, do not double that amount—unless inflation has increased 100 percent since this book has been published.

We hope this book will help parents to relax and see their children realistically. We hope parents will learn to guide their children successfully through the positive elements in their community and protect them from the negative and destructive elements. We hope parents will learn who has reliable information and who does not, who will help them and who will hurt them.

If this book has the influence within the family and between the family and the community that we believe is possible, then happier families will indeed result.

2 The Community

Parents and the Community

As pointed out in Chapter 1, a major thrust of this book derives from the authors' experience that other factors besides the parent-child relationship are of great significance in the child's development. These include sociological factors beyond a parent's control, such as the influence of the school and other community facilities and agencies, peer influences, and the temperamental makeup of the child.

Prior to the 1960s, as pointed out in Chapter 1, parents could count upon community factors and influences as relatively steady, unchanging, and reflecting values similar to those taught in the home. As a result, the proper focus of the child-rearing was in the relationship between the parent and child.

When one thought of child-rearing problems and practices, he was concerned mainly with the relationships within the family itself and could take community and "outside" influences pretty much for granted. Recently, more and more individuals and institutions outside of the family have taken it upon themselves to introduce value systems to the child that they feel are superior to those of the family and, therefore, in many cases in conflict with traditional values taught within the family.

Humanism

A review of recent child-rearing books indicates that two primary systems are now in vogue. One is the human-growth and encounter-group movement, emphasizing communications and facilitation of feeling, which seems to identify with modern humanism and stresses the importance of man and of man's dignity; man's innate worth should command respect. Man is seen as valuable no matter what he has or has not done.

There are certainly some positive things about this philosophy, but there are some drawbacks if it is improperly applied to children. For example, to respect a person who cannot achieve is one thing, but it should not follow that we do away with competition so that those who can achieve are prevented from gaining recognition for their success. Such thinking has led to school report cards that are difficult to interpret because achievement and competition are not emphasized.

The problems associated with this approach were illustrated by a Dallas, Texas, report card. Dallas parents and children were given an 8½-by-14-inch number-filled sheet that looked more like a page from a company audit than a report card. To assist them in deciphering the report, which was used for kindergarten through third grade, pupils' parents were supplied with a thirty-two page booklet called "When Your Child Starts School" and a twenty-eight page manual with the remarkable title "Terminal Behavioral Objectives for Continuous Progression Modules in Early Childhood Education." Later it was necessary to hire a free-lance writer to write yet another supplementary pamphlet to explain the explanation.

Secondly, while this group teaches that children have feelings just like their parents, we believe children do not have the intelligence or judgment of adults. For this reason, they should not be responsible for planning their own academic programs or running their own schools.

This group also frowns on competition and achievement. Yet successful people in our society usually achieve their success through competition. How do they propose youth acquire this essential characteristic of competition when competition is not only neglected in the schools, but when children who are encouraged at home to compete are also often unrewarded in the schools because they are considered out of place?

Part of this humanistic credo holds that discipline and structure undoubtedly have self-discipline as a primary characteristic. Strong discipline and structure are present in the backgrounds of successful people. How does this humanist propose that a person acquire these characteristics?

This group teaches and lives by the tenet that all people are of equal worth or value. All people are not of equal worth or value. If this were true, why should one be concerned with improving one's self? Why work so hard to be successful, make money, live in a certain neighborhood, or country? Since we do not live as if all people are of equal worth in our society as adults, why should we oblige our children to learn a different set of values that must be *unlearned* for them to be successful adults themselves? Often this "unlearning process" is a tense, difficult, and occasionally tragic time in the life of a young adult.

As a corollary to the "all people are of equal worth and value" tenet, the humanist tells us that it is important for children to rub shoulders with and learn the behavior and values of all other children. That the more aggressive, less happy, discourteous, and nonscholastically oriented first and second grader can learn positive characteristics from the child who is polite, calm, and an achiever may be true. But that is a two-way street.

Why should the parent who works hard and diligently to raise his children properly, with strong, constructive values, allow the schools to determine that other behavior is as acceptable and as permissible? What a task parents are faced with when their eight-year-old comes home with language, attitudes, and behavior that the child did not learn at home but that seem acceptable at school. The child is confused, the parent is confused, and the system is confused. What do children have in common with life-styles that are so different from those of their families, and why should the young child not become confused by alternate styles of life when his or her own life-style is not yet solidified?

Many Americans who matured during the 1960s, when many traditional standards of behavior and morality were challenged, now appear to be experiencing increasing frustration, anxiety, and depression. There is an increase in the number of people in their late twenties and early thirties receiving psychiatric help, according to various mental health experts and statistics compiled by the National Center for Health Statistics. And this is confirmed by our own clinical experience.

The authors believe that these humanistic principles can be of value to some parents. They encourage people to get closer to their feelings and to be more sensitive to the feelings of their spouses and others. The human growth movement has also made it respectable for individuals to seek counseling and self-improvement without the stigma attached to psychological therapy. It can also make a parent more aware of a child's feelings, and the emphasis of humanism and the Gestalt movement on physical touching is certainly an important one in relating to children.

Some adults become overly involved in this theory, however, and do not balance its emphasis on feelings with an equal emphasis on reason and behavior. Some parents not only use these tools for their own self-development but also embrace the entire philosophy with little awareness of the general values implicit in this brand of humanism.

This theory creates the most difficulties when the parent forces the child to accept this philosophy, and the young child is forced to adopt a humanistic life-style. This system seems to emphasize the importance of the individual, as opposed to institutions such as church, family, and community, so that the child is put into a position of criticizing and downgrading the structure provided by these institutions that are so important to him. This can prove quite confusing for the child. It raises many anxieties and brings the child into conflict and confrontation with traditional institutions before he is capable of evaluating the pros and cons of these institutions and their necessity in society.

The adult who has embraced some of the positive humanistic principles for himself and who would like his children to develop these characteristics of awareness of feelings and development of self would be wise to consider the possibility that his children will be more likely to develop these positive characteristics if given structure as a child.

Existential self-awareness and responsibility toward self are admirable ideals that many adults pursue without success during their entire adult lives. To overexpose children to these sophisticated ideals will only lead to anxiety and a misinterpretation of the responsibilities inherent in this life-style.

The emphasis on communications in this humanism can also be confusing, and some children are led to believe that as long as they communicate a great deal about their behavior they have the "freedom" to participate in any type of behavior they wish. Children and their parents sometimes reach faulty conclusions in their thinking. They state that feelings are of primary importance, and because rules and regulations impede the expression of these feelings at times, rules are blamed for obstructing the child's growth. Actually these individuals seem to be confusing feelings and reasoning. You will hear such statements as "I *feel* that teachers should not give grades in my school." This is not a feeling but an intellectual opinion that has been couched in humanistic (feeling) terminology.

In this manner, the humanist can beget a "tyranny of shoulds" just as his puritanical ancestor did. These individuals can impose very rigid sets of rules for others (and these others are almost always above them in society's prestige scale), becoming quite upset when others do not conform to their philosophy. They then state that other people are not open to their communications. Perhaps this is just human frailty, because it is always easier to impose a "tyranny of shoulds" on others than on oneself.

Another danger in this humanistic approach is that the principles involved are in an embryonic stage, and it is always dangerous to experiment on humans with new systems and practices. It is one thing for an adult to seek growth through this philosophy: He is taking his own risks. But it is quite another thing to impose this system on children in school.

It is rather difficult to see why so many public school systems have chosen to implement this approach on their young charges, but this can probably be traced to many teacher training programs at universities. It is of interest that many of the humanists are the first to pronounce themselves as opponents of human exploitation, especially of children.

Unfortunately, school systems seem destined to implement whatever seems new, crisp, and exciting. We will probably continue to see new systems tested on our children, including rational-emotive therapy, transactional analysis, transcendental meditation (TM), and behavior modification approaches.

Behavior Modification

Behavior modification is another system that is currently popular and, like humanism, has many positive and negative attributes. Behavior modification derives primarily from learning theory and animal research rather than work with emotionally disturbed individuals, as is the case with humanism. Behavior modification has proved effective in changing behavior patterns and in breaking habits that are disturbing to the individual and seen as socially unacceptable to others. The same questions arise here, however, and relate to who is implementing these techniques, on whom, and for what purpose. While humanism emphasizes emotions and communications, behavior modification stresses behavior change.

Behavior modification theory and technique can help parents to be more aware of their own behavior and how it affects others, and it can increase the parents' awareness of cause and effect relationships and how these affect the child. It can make the parent more aware of how he or she might unwittingly be teaching the child socially undesirable behavior patterns. The authors have seen parents who have gone overboard in adopting behavior modification techniques, and these parents respond to their children as though they are robots, rewarding them with a piece of gum or candy following each socially positive behavior. While such an approach can provide structure and security for the younger child, who certainly needs structure, it can—when used in the extreme —implicitly downplay the importance of feelings, communication, and self-direction.

Some of the recent criticism of behavior modification comes from the humanistic school. Humanists do not argue with the effectiveness of behavior modification techniques in cases of severe retardation, autism, learning disabilities, and toilet training. They do object to these methods when they are used to control "healthy" populations in schools, businesses, towns, and society in general. Many humanists feel that free will is the major factor separating man from lesser forms of life and that behavioral control could effectively stamp out man's humanness by robbing him of his free will.

And recent studies conducted by psychologists indicate that "chocolate candy magic" may fade rather fast. The reward of tokens (candies, points, pennies, stars) for desired behavior may not teach different behaviors but rather how to earn tokens. Some research now indicates that changes in behavior are not maintained long once tokens are withdrawn. Instead of promoting interest in a specific learning activity, external rewards may actually decrease interest in an activity even if the activity is interesting and enjoyable on its own.

When one looks at the weaknesses inherent in the extremes of both humanism and behavior modification, the analogy of the growth of a plant comes to mind. In order for a plant to grow it must begin as a healthy seed with reasonably healthy soil and the requirements of proper water, air, light, and nutrients. The naive humanist (as opposed to the mature individual who may use components of the humanistic school) is much like a well-meaning child who plants the seed in an open and unprotected area where it will have the "freedom" it needs to develop. The child then overtends the plant pouring on great amounts of water and great amounts of fertilizer. The plant is then subjected to strong winds, lashing rains, and excessive heat before it is strong enough and mature enough to cope with these elements. It may take on a sudden spurt and appear overly developed for a short time before it withers.

The naive behaviorist (as opposed to a mature person who uses behavioristic principles) is like the child who protects the plant and ensures its growth by placing it in a very protected environment and interwinding it in a lattice so that it will have a great amount of structure. The plant grows but never reaches its full potential and its direction and shape is determined to a large extent by the gardener who grows it according to his own design.

If these child-rearing systems have so many drawbacks then what

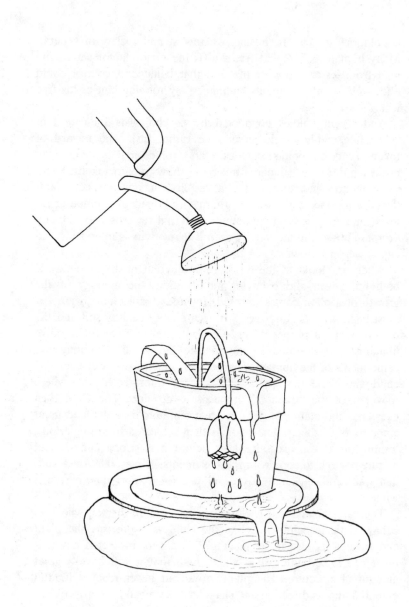

system should be used in rearing children? The authors feel that children are too complex to be pigeonholed in a particular theory. Almost all child-rearing systems can provide some useful information to aid parents, as long as parents do not naively accept the entire system and are aware of the weaknesses and values inherent in each system. Parents must also be highly aware of the influence of institutions within the community and help their child weave through the sociological maze of opportunities and obstacles provided by the community. These community influences have a much greater effect on the child today than they did twenty years ago. (See Figures 1 and 2.)

Because of the reduced influence of parents and the greater influence of peers and community institutions today, it is even more essential that parents dedicate themselves to helping their children while they are young and while they are amenable to parental values.

While it is important for children to have leisure time in the home, it is of great importance that parents be available to interact, respond, and teach their children. If parents find that they are unable to spend time with their children because of many other activities and community responsibilities, they should make a list of the activities that interfere with parenting so they will know which things they value more than their children.

Rules, Reason, and Emotion

Parents must also be aware of the *developmental principle,* which is elaborated upon later in this book. There are three main areas of consideration here: rules, reason, and emotion. In the child's early age ranges, parents will teach the child more through rules and structure than through reasoning. At later ages there will be a balance between the use of of rules, reason, and pointing out emotional implications in teaching the child values. The parents must also be aware that these three areas make up different proportions of the child's experience as he grows. In early age ranges, the child is more purely emotional. Later he or she develops an even balance between feelings, reasoning, and structure.

The authors hope the following chapters will provide guidelines

Figure 1. Proportion of Influence on a Child in the 1950s

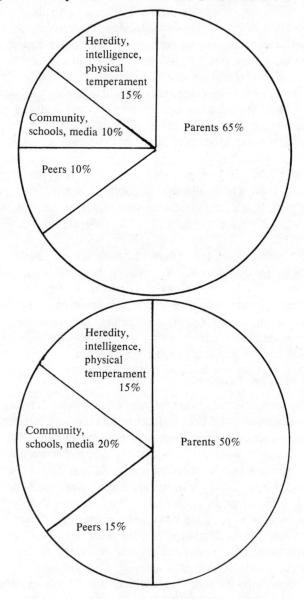

Figure 2. Proportion of Influence on a Child in the 1970s

and expectations that will help parents understand their children and treat them as unique individuals. Becoming an outstanding parent requires dedication and an awareness of the child's positive qualities. While not manipulating, parents must provide structure for their children. Reasonable expectations at home and in the community are important. The chart of approximate standards (Table 1) can be useful in serving as a guideline for some expectations.

The chart is not exact and will change, of course, with changes in the economy and society. It does provide a rough guideline, however, and one can make exceptions to it in order to suit individual occasions and unique circumstances.

The reader will note in reviewing the chart that children's allowances are given freely and not attached to any particular responsibility. Children should receive allowances simply because they are children and because they need an opportunity to learn to regulate and save money. To do that they should not be completely dependent upon parents for each expenditure. It will also be noted that children are expected to perform responsibilities without pay or other reward because they are members of the household and have obligations just as their parents have obligations. Additional wages can be earned for work over and above that required as a part of family participation.

Some parents will be surprised to note the recommendations that the seventeen-, eighteen-, and nineteen-year-old child is still given a weekly allowance. Such an allowance might not be necessary if the child were employed. Other parents will be surprised to see a weekly curfew on the nineteen-year-old. While this person is an adult in the legal sense, he or she should still have respect for the harmony and life-style of the family if residing in the home. Others will be surprised to see a required minimum amount of nonproductive time, but the authors have seen some children who, to their detriment, have been placed on recreational, academic, and achievement schedules that would tax the endurance of an adult. Some of these children are pressured to such an extent that they have virtually no relaxation or private nonproductive time.

Table 1. Approximate Standards

Age	Responsibilities per Day / Work Time per Week	Wages for Work Hours (No Payment for Responsibilities)*	Weekly Allowance	Weekly Savings and Contributions (Church, etc.)	Money Kept by Child from Gifts for Pleasure (Balance Goes to Savings)*	Bedtime (P.M.) School	Summer	Weekend	Weekly Curfews	Maximum Average Nightly Homework Time in Hours	Minimum Average Daily Leisure Time in Hours	Maximum Daily T.V. Time in Hours
2-5	None	None	None	None	$ .10	When Child Is Tired				0	5	1.5
6	2	$ .05 per ½ Hour	None	None	.10	7:30	7:30	7:30		0	5	1.5
7	2	.10	$ .35	None	.50	8:00	8:30	8:30		0	5	1.5
8	2	.15	.45	None	.50	8:00	9:00	9:00		.33	2½	2
9	3	.20	.55	$ .05	1.00	8:30	9:30	9:30		.50	2½	2.5
	½ Hour											
10	3	.30	.65	.10	1.00	9:00	10:00	10:00		.75	2½	3
	½ Hour											

11	3	½ Hour	.35	.90	.10	1.00	9:00	10:30	10:30		1	2½	3
12	3	½ Hour	.40	1.20	.15	1.00	9:30	11:00	11:00		1.5	2	3.5
13	3	1 Hour	.90	1.65	.25	3.00	10:00	11:30	12:00		2	2	3.5
14	3	1 Hour	1.00	2.25	.30	3.00	10:30	Self-Regulated			2	2	3.5
15	3	1 Hour	1.10	2.75	.35	4.00	10:30	Self-Regulated	Self-Regulated	1 Night 9:00*	2	2	3.5
16	3	2 Hours	1.25	4.00	.65	5.00	11:00	Self-Regulated		2 Nights 9:30 / 2 Nights 11:00*	2	1½	Self-Regulated
17	3	2 Hours	1.35	5.00	.75	10.00	11:00	Self-Regulated		2 Nights 12:30 / 5 Nights 10.30	2	1½	Self-Regulated
18	3	2 Hours	1.50	6.00	.85	ALL	11:30	Self-Regulated		2 Nights 1:00 / 5 Nights 11:30	Self-Regulated	1	Self-Regulated
19+	3	2 Hours	1.50	8.00	1.00	ALL	11:30	Self-Regulated		1:30	Self-Regulated	1	Self-Regulated

*Subject to increases in cost of living   *Later for supervised group situations

21

Parental Rights

Both parents and children have rights. Parents should not feel guilty for being human. If parents are sick, they sometimes cannot fulfill a commitment they have previously made with the child, and these are natural occurrences in the family.

The family is not in the fullest sense a democracy, and parents and children are not on the same level in all areas. If parents give a child the same responsibility for decision-making that they give themselves, they can very easily produce an anxious or fearful child.

At the same time, children do need the opportunity to exert control but in considerably more circumscribed areas. For example, children can be responsible for the arrangement of their own rooms, for scheduling their free time, and for spending their own limited money.

Parents should not feel guilty because they do not experience life in the same way that their nine-year-old child does, for example. Parents should not fully participate or fully agree with their children and it should be understood that children are not asking to share fully or necessarily be fully agreed with by their parents. They are asking for the freedom to exercise themselves in limited ways, not to be rejected or neglected but rather respected and permitted.

Many times parents who reject children force them to rebel. It is also true that parents who fully agree with anything their children desire, drive these children further from reality and middle-class values into absurdities. Perhaps we can learn from history in this area: The reader may remember that his or her father would never have worn blue suede shoes or pegged pants with zippers at the cuffs and clearly stated the position of nonapproval for himself. However, he may have permitted his children to wear some of this clothing in circumscribed situations.

Responsibilities and Freedom

The area of parental rights also includes expectations for responsibilities on the part of children. Children should be obliged to make beds, carry out garbage, watch over younger siblings, and behave themselves. Decisions in the areas of education, bedtime, timing of meals, choice of friends, the nature of discipline, the range of recreational resources, and vacations should be left largely to the parents' authority. On the other hand, children can be given the responsibility for circumscribed decisions concerning interests, hobbies, spare time, and monetary expenditures. Naturally, the age of the child must be considered in terms of the decision involved.

This does not mean that unified family goals or commitments are ruled out. They can certainly be important in limited areas such as picnics, family movie outings, or family games.

Parents should also enjoy freedom from their children on occasion and freedom from each other. Emancipation in marriage is perhaps as vital as union in marriage. It is of the utmost importance that children see unity in their parents; however, they must also see their parents as capable of independence from each other and from them.

It can be very important for parents with young children to occasionally get away from the children, and this is especially true of the mother, who is usually the primary caretaker. It is often important for a mother to get away with her husband to a place that is ordered and uncluttered and where she is not responsible for preparing meals or discharging maternal obligations. Unfortunately, parents are usually in a better financial position to take these kinds of short trips after the children are older and when the necessity for this kind of relief for the mother is not as urgent.

Family mealtimes are not as sacred as one might believe. If the children are rather active and disruptive at meals, especially at early ages, the parents might be wise to eat occasional meals by themselves after the children are fed.

Grandparents and other relatives can occasionally intrude in unacceptable ways into the primary family sphere. While it is hoped that grandparents will have earned respect and can add important experiences and values for the family, they should not be allowed to disrupt the family unit. The family unit must remain husband-wife and children, periodically expanding to include grandparents and often close relatives.

Expectations

Parental expectations are crucial and necessary and change at different stages of child development. If a parent's expectations are too high and the children cannot perform to meet these expectations, the parent can become disappointed, frustrated, and angry at the children. The children in turn may respond with frustration of their own, resulting in a lowered self-concept. But if parental expectations are too low, achievement will be lowered and much of the child's performance may go unnoticed by the parent and, therefore, unrewarded. The result here is also disappointment and perhaps the feeling of parental neglect on the child's part. Unrealistically high expectations for a child can lead to some feelings of rejection; extremely low expectations can result in feelings of neglect.

Values

Children need their parents desperately to help them develop moral values and principles. Parents who do not guide their child in the development of adequate moral values and principles are not permitting the child's conscience to develop appropriately. Such children may very well develop difficulties later in moral behavior and in understanding the appropriate value system required in honest business and professional work. Parents need to teach their children and guide them through the formative years—the years of rapid development. If parents let go too quickly, trouble can occur.

The issue of freedom is often bantered about and an increasing percentage of young people today are insisting that they are "more free" than their parents were. Changed life-styles, improved transportation, and media systems have surely given youth more freedom of action, movement, and information. It is clear, however, that the freest people in our society are those who are successful in whatever work they do. In effect, they have "purchased" their freedom during their working and leisure hours, and the community permits them considerably more latitude in their behavior and, therefore, their freedom. On the other hand, many a youth who claims he is "free" may not be free at all. He may continue to attempt to influence other people to his way for life, yet the community rarely permits him the freedom that he claims he has already taken. The community is critical and restrictive of individuals who demand unearned freedom. This is simply a case of the minority of our youth being confused about freedom. In a sense they are "copping out" in regard to hard work to attempt to achieve the true freedom that our business, professional, and community leaders have earned.

Some areas of our society appear to be sliding away from many of the traditional values that have been so vital to our society. These changes appear to be aided in some cases by the popular press, the underground press, the values of the university, and the awarding of too much responsibility and decision-making to young adults. It is difficult to tell how extensive this movement is, but many parents of the 1970s are faced with people selling the concept either real or mythical that "times have changed."

One can observe a general cynicism regarding America, its traditions, its history, its cornerstones of philosophy. We can watch television and observe a professional athlete turn his back on the American flag during the national anthem. We can watch fans at football games chatting among themselves during the same anthem. We see schools giving children the option of saying the pledge of allegiance to the flag and our churches frequently denying the relevance of ancient traditions that have guided them for thousands of years. We can see the effect of this cynicism in the family when there is a rejection of family values that have proved through the generations to be essential to family unity and integrity. This cynicism can drive a wedge into the American family and make it impotent as a guiding force.

A second "nouveau" value is the rejection of history. All we need do is observe many of our "new" federal, state, and local programs to realize that little or no concern is given to what predecessors in the community have observed. Things need to be new, innovative, crisp, and entirely relevant to current times. The wisdom as well as the nature of the errors of our ancestors are lost when history is neglected.

It is ironic, indeed, to witness the increasing number of people who turn to the psychologist for guidance regarding values and morality after their approach to the clergy has resulted in shallow and amoral psychological interpretations of their problems.

It would appear that present-day psychology and psychiatry still generally maintain a hostility to the inhibitory message of traditional morality and religion. This hostility has permeated the teaching of many college undergraduates and increasing numbers of high school and elementary school pupils as new, "pop psychology" approaches are implemented in the public school system.

Dr. Donald T. Campbell of Northwestern University, formerly president of the American Psychological Association, stated that "on purely scientific grounds the recipes for living that have been evolved, tested, and winnowed through hundreds of generations of human social history might be regarded as better tested than the best of psychology's and psychiatry's speculations on how lives should be lived."

Separation of church and state is an underlying principle in the United States Constitution, and one might question the role of the public school in teaching these so-called alternative life-styles and value systems that have been described as new religions or at least competing value systems. Because it is really impossible to avoid teaching values, it would appear that the most authentic question has to do with which values will be taught to elementary and secondary schoolchildren in our public schools.

Perhaps another way of approaching that question is to ask whether the value changes of society and resultant goals are to be set by mature adults who have been taught the basic skills in school and who have an appreciation of history and societal functions or by social scientists, teachers, and students simply out of the framework of social science technology.

Home Location and Design

Ideally, a home will be near a good public school and a well-established private school. The private school may be used to fall back on during various stages in the child's development. Public schools in which more than 25 percent of the school population comes from the lower socioeconomic class should be approached with caution, since this mix may pull down the achievement level within the school. Student leadership may then deteriorate as some children are moved to private schools to avoid social and academic problems.

The nature of living space within the home is extremely important, and problems of lack of privacy can develop. Noise level within the home should be low. Many modern homes tend toward open spaces and breeziness at the expense of privacy and separation.

Many homes are poorly designed for child-rearing. For example, the kitchen is often separated from the family room by only a counter. This results in a high noise level coming from the dishwasher, television set, stereo, etc. An older type of home may be a better investment for child-rearing purposes because it provides a more insulated foundation and greater privacy and separation of rooms.

Ideally, each home should have a recreation room that is not a "family room" but rather a ten-by-twelve-foot or larger room where handicrafts may be kept and various types of experimentation with tools and construction toys can take place.

Parents should not only be aware of and try to reduce such environmental factors as noise and lack of privacy within the home, but they should also be cognizant of the times of the day when more stress is evident. For example, in the six to nine year age range, the thirty-minute period prior to attending school in the morning might prove to be a stressful one along with the period between five and six o'clock in the evening when the child is hungry and fatigued from a full day of activities. Another stressful time is prior to bedtime. By recognizing that there might be only a few critical times during the day when tempers flare, parents can often forestall them through a conscientious effort to modify interactions. For example, some mothers awaken very slowly in the morning. Everyone's interests would be better served if no one attempted to be cheerful and friendly and if the father and children knew this was not a time to engage in lengthy conversations involving decision-making.

If possible, homes should be chosen near a central complex of recreation areas, shops, and schools so that children can walk to activities and reduce the "chauffeuring" problem experienced by mothers. Cities with a population of less than 30,0000 offer many advantages for child-rearing compared with the suburbs of large cities and large cities themselves. Children can be allowed more freedom in a smaller community, and there are fewer problems with school integration, busing, and crime. If possible, parents should choose a house in a neighborhood where children of the same age live. A neighborhood with a great number of very young children or elderly people should be avoided because the family that is "different" can become isolated from or rejected by the neighborhood.

There are many other advantages to living in a small town. Children are able to walk from one part of town to another, meeting acquaintances and having something to keep them occupied. In addition, the lack of anonymity in a small town creates social awareness and exerts pressure for correct behavior. The norms and values of the community are supported in many ways as the child walks or rides his bicycle through the community. The family-owned hardware store, the local ice cream parlor, the library, and other facilities of this type are usually positive forces in a child's development. These businesses and institutions are helpful not because of the nature of the work carried on there but because the people who run them are local and known in the community. The neighborhood grocery store, hamburger stand, and drugstore are a far cry from the current impersonal franchises found in most areas of large cities.

In many larger cities, mass-transit systems are usually under-developed so that children are virtually imprisoned in their own neighborhood, unless a parent dons a chauffeur's cap or complex car pools are arranged. Some larger suburbs in southern areas of the United States do not even provide sidewalks, so that intra-neighborhood contact and communications for youth are reduced. In certain areas, jobs for teens are frequently difficult to find, and recreation centers in many areas are poorly staffed.

Boredom is a significant contributor to drug use, delinquency, and other behavioral problems in middle-class children. City administrators need to see the importance of jobs, recreational facilities, and mass transportation systems as crucial factors in aiding the development of healthy and well-adjusted youth. A healthy and well-adjusted nucleus of youth in a community can exert more positive peer pressure on young people who have developed problems than can all of the "crisis centers" that are neatly designed by federal and state bureaucrats for the minority of troubled children.

This same type of approach can be extremely valuable in the school community where school counselors can develop and reward the personal strengths of their students and study the positive and negative effects of peer groups, rather than concentrating exclusively on psychological counseling for a minority of students who may not respond to this form of therapy. Through the years the authors have observed that rewarding hard-working students by grades, certificates, exemptions from final examinations, and even the right to miss classes can be more effective in developing positive peer pressure for the entire high school system than can "rap" groups, student rights groups, or smoking lounges.

Schools and the Community

Most parents are aware of the enormous problems facing our public schools today. They are aware of the increased delinquency, truancy, discipline problems, and low achievement. As mentioned previously in this book, changes in institutions such as the school require the parent of today to be more aware of the community institutions that affect his child. This was not the case in the 1940s and 1950s when the values of the school matched those of the middle-class parent closely.

Are parents to blame for their children's problems in school? Recent newspaper article headlines would appear to fix much of the blame on parents: "DRUGS, PARENT LACK OF INTEREST, AND DISCIPLINE ARE THE MAJOR PROBLEMS IN THE SCHOOL SYSTEM." "LACK OF PARENTAL CONTROL BLAMED." "SCHOOL PROBLEMS

BLAMED ON ADULTS' ATTITUDES." "PARENTS ARE TO BLAME NOT
ONLY FOR DISCIPLINE PROBLEMS, BUT ALSO FOR ACHIEVEMENT
PROBLEMS."

Goals

The authors have seen few parents who are guilty of these
charges. We believe many other factors are involved. Prior to the
1950s, public education was concerned with preparing youth for
business, the trades, or college. In the 1950s, after the Russians
launched Sputnik, achievement centered on science and mathematics; then in the 1960s an attempt was made to eliminate poverty and racial discrimination. Now it seems that we are entering
a phase of humanism in which each child will be understood and
given a "global" type of education. Educational goals are constantly changing, and these changes disturb and confuse many
of the parents seen by the authors. Parents are upset not only by
achievement problems but also about the social values that are
taught—or not taught—in the public schools.

Educational Techniques

Secondly, educational techniques keep changing. Educators
experiment with our children to test new theories. We have seen
these changing techniques lower the morale of many teachers,
however, and reduce the stability the child needs. After all, a
child is constantly changing on the inside, and the younger the
child the more he is changing within himself. This calls for *more*
structure on the outside. Thus when there is constant change on
the outside, it can be difficult for the child.

If you do not have structure you do not have tradition. A March
11, 1974, article in the *Wall Street Journal* reported that a leading
American university president visited Oxford University and found
the Oxford president in his office reading Aristotle. The American
administrator asked his counterpart how he could manage the university and have time for contemplative study. His answer was
"tradition."

Changing techniques make tradition difficult to achieve and
sustain, and the period between 1962 and 1972 has been called the

age of innovation in public education. The Ford Foundation conducted a study of the $30 million it contributed to educational programs and found these programs resulted in no significant elevation in academic skills. The United States Office of Education reported that money from foundations went mainly into the following kinds of programs during those ten years: Team teaching, modular scheduling, nongraded schools, programmed learning, individualized instructions, computer-assisted instructions, independent study, learning centers, "open" schools, language laboratories, behavioral objectives, and differentiated staffing. While these changes have caused many problems, we keep hearing about newer innovations to come.

When parents in one community objected to the falling achievement scores in a new middle-school program, for example, they were admonished by the principal that new tests would be designed to measure improvements in student self-concept. That was where much of the effort of the faculty was put. And rapid changes and innovations have led to the collapse of some schools. A case in point is the William Tyndale School in London, England. Within two years after the introduction of various innovative programs, the William Tyndale School had deteriorated, and striking teachers, angry parents, and helpless politicians were confronting one another as reported in the English press.

A reason commonly given for the various innovative programs is to accommodate many types of children within one educational system. It would appear, on the basis of recent experiences, that school officials may need to acknowledge that some individuals are less intelligent and less motivated than others. Attempts to educate all children within the school are necessary, but not when the degree of time and effort prohibits the more intelligent and better adjusted child from reaching full potential.

One innovation apparently designed to correct recent excesses is the so-called fundamental or traditional school. While these schools emphasize basic skills as well as discipline, it is hoped that educational advances in teaching and curriculum outside of the basic skills will not be "thrown out with the bath water."

Isn't it sad that a traditional school concept had to be developed as a new and innovative approach before an emphasis on academics could be reintroduced to academia? How unfortunate that many public school administrators suffer from an intellectual selfishness that has insulated them from the repeated stated desires of parents and the general public. Private schools may indeed be more public than the "privately" administered public schools, in many cases.

A third factor affecting public schools is size itself, and the consolidation of facilities. Consolidation seems to solve some problems because it appears to be less expensive. But certainly there are some problems inherent in size and consolidation of schools. Assume 5 percent of the children in a school have "problems." In a school of five hundred students, that means you have twenty-five students who may create disciplinary problems. If you have a school of fifteen hundred students, you are now talking about seventy-five problem children, a number sufficient for a small riot. Also, we have observed that students become disorganized with large consolidated plants. They are noisy and there is less supervision and personal attention.

Integration has certainly caused disciplinary and achievement problems. When large numbers of lower socioeconomic class students were abruptly moved into middle-class public schools, parents became anxious. Problems in both achievement and discipline occurred, as evidenced by many school riots and the declining achievement levels of schoolchildren.

Departure of as many as 10 to 15 percent of students in some counties to private schools has damaged public schools because there is nothing stronger than peer pressure to develop either positive or negative social values. And when you take out some of the achieving students, you leave a gap that is difficult to fill. Of course, the support from all of the parents of children in private schools are also lost to the public schools. It is unfortunate that parental attitude research accomplished by the public schools often does not include parents who have children in private schools. This is analogous to the Pepsi-Cola Company trying to research its product and only making inquiries of people who drink Pepsi and not those who drink Dr. Pepper or 7-Up.

While the goal of integration is to provide equal opportunities in terms of curriculum, social interactions, and mental-health programs, the authors have observed what appears to be segregation within schools continuing in many areas. Recent studies and observations indicate that there is a preponderance of middle-class and upper middle-class children who are invited into programs for the gifted and remedial programs for the learning disabled child. At the same time, a preponderance of lower socioeconomic and minority children appear to be routed toward special truancy programs and child abuse programs. The American Civil Liberties Union has charged that government programs for prevention and treatment of child abuse are aimed almost entirely at poor families, which results in many of these children being taken from their families and placed in foster care. The contention of the ACLU is that foster care is more damaging to these lower socioeconomic children than leaving them in their natural homes, in most cases.

As mentioned previously, humanism presents another factor that may adversely affect the schools. The underlying humanistic philosophy tends to downplay the importance of competition and achievement while emphasizing the feelings of the child. In addition, elementary age children are encouraged to make many academic decisions beyond their judgment and experience. This insistence that children become their own masters at an early age (and many humanists are rigid in requiring the child to conform to this philosophy) can teach children to discount the authority of a teacher while they "do their own thing." Children often move blissfully along until they reach junior high and high school, where many of our public schools have a different approach and expect children to settle down and get to work. Could it be that many of the disciplinary problems in junior high and high school are caused by the public schools' own laissez-faire philosophy in the early grades?

Interestingly enough, from a developmental point of view, this seems to be handled in reverse order. It is the younger child who needs greater structure and the older child who can begin to experience and develop independent thinking and interests and contribute to the policies of a school in a more democratic way. It is ironic indeed to consider that the humanistic approach in the early grades may be resulting in totalitarian approaches at the high-school level, where principals may overreact in order to maintain discipline and where greater financial expenditures are made every day for police security forces.

An example of the humanistic approach in the classroom was reported in the October 1, 1973, St. Petersburg *Times*. The article described a "magic circle" technique, which grows out of self-actualization thought. "A small group of fourth, fifth and sixth graders were asked questions by their leader like 'Which rules would you like to change about our school?' and 'What would you like to change about our school?' Then the leader switched to a value clarification query: 'What would you take with you if you had to move suddenly?' Finally, the group was over and the children jumped up, put away their chairs, turned the phonograph on loud, helped themselves to cookies and punch, and a party began." The article stated that twelve-year-old Michael, the leader, conducted this session "with the ease of a professional."

This type of report certainly appears exciting and impressive on the surface, but research by G. Zivin, reported in *Today's Child,* January, 1975, indicates that encouraging young children to talk and think about particular objects actually reduces rather than increases interest in that particular object. The authors are of the opinion that group discussion usually increases interest in a subject area. The other possibility is pointed out here to demonstrate once again the limitations of social science programs that have not been supported by experience, history, and research over a sufficient length of time.

There are other tenets or implications of the human-growth school: discipline and structure are stifling to the individual, all institutions—including the family—are suspect, education and other publicly supported groups must take over the parenting function, everyone is equal in intelligence and differences in intelligence must be the fault of parents. Finally, humanists believe that communications solve all problems.

While humanism and existentialism can be very valuable, we must be careful about how they are implemented in the schools, especially with younger children. Certainly, the idea that children should respect themselves may be a very good one and we should have programs that stress the development of self-respect. But we have to look at priorities in terms of what children are learning or not learning in school. The saying some humanists have of "do your own thing" is all right if you know what your "own" is. And that takes experience in living.

Overpopulation is a problem that we have attempted to solve through consolidation of buildings and construction of large schools. We may think this approach saves money, but if we deducted the expense of special workers, disciplinary teams, and school psychologists who attempt to deal with the problems created by these large complexes, perhaps smaller schools would appear more feasible. Perhaps our business and community leaders could help us achieve smaller school units in an economical way.

Significantly, the regulation of local school matters takes place at state and national levels to some extent. School boards must look for federally funded programs that approximate what the local administration would like to accomplish. They do not know when or if they will receive the money. Many teachers are trained at state universities with departments of education highly influenced by social scientists who may never have taught in the classroom, or who are trying out new theories, or who may not share the values of the people who live in a particular community. As a result, the problems of many local school districts may originate at the state universities.

A recent study in Los Angeles involving a ten-year assessment of factors influencing pupil school performance has concluded that children's success or failure in reading is largely determined by the quality of their teachers' training. A study at the University of California concluded that "arguments about the influence of Mom and Dad and their education, poverty, and neighborhood can no longer be used as excuses for a child not learning to read." One of the main reasons for students' reading problems is that they are in over their heads and, so the study indicated, are many teachers.

A study in Philadelphia conducted by the Federal Reserve Bank traced the academic development of 1,896 pupils in one hundred fifty Philadelphia schools over two-and-one-half years. The factors most closely related to pupil achievement appeared to include the quality of the undergraduate college attended by the teacher as well as class size, school size, and teacher's classroom experience.

A study conducted at the State University College in New York indicates that reading lessons belong in the curriculum well beyond elementary school; yet not many qualified reading teachers teach at the secondary school level. The poll of more than a thousand four year colleges and universities indicated that more than 80 percent of future high-school teachers are not required to take even a basic reading methods course.

Public schools have family-life courses. These courses can, depending upon how they are handled, represent a further intrusion into the family. One only hopes that the teachers of these courses will have raised *successful* families of their own. It is again ironical that these courses are offered as a way of helping children learn about family life. The implication is that parents have done a poor job in disciplining the child. In fact, the school system itself may have eroded this discipline in many ways.

Of course, not all public schools have problems, and public schools vary a great deal in quality just as do private schools. Some public schools seem not to feel the shock waves of constant innovation and change. Some of the better public schools seem to have been able to offer more durable programs because their architectural design has not been amenable to open space and other innovative concepts. Unfortunately, parents are rarely able to send their children to the public school of their choice. It is unconstitutional. In some districts it is possible for parents to pay to have their child attend the public school of choice, but this is not true everywhere.

It is important that the child receive a good basic foundation in the primary skills of reading, spelling, and arithmetic. If the local public school is not emphasizing these skills, and if discipline is poor, the parent may well decide to send the child to a private school during the early grades.

How does a parent evaluate a child's achievement in school?

Most public and private schools publish results of the child's group achievement testing in school. These tests usually compare the child with children from all over the United States or with children within the same school or school system. If the child is achieving somewhat above national norms, and the teacher feels he or she is working up to potential, then there is usually little about which to be concerned.

If the child is achieving below national norms, the parent may wish to have the child tested by a psychologist to determine achievement level relative to intellectual ability. The group achievement tests in schools do not usually measure many of the skills necessary for performance in the classroom such as writing speed, auditory memory for directions, and other such functional skills. Thus, it is possible for a child to be at or above national norms and still be a source of concern to his teacher. Some very bright children with learning disabilities are only able to achieve at grade level and this might be several grade levels below their potential.

Another area of concern is the junior high school or middle school. Children of this age are highly subject to peer pressure and to a great deal of change in themselves as they enter adolescence. There is growing evidence that drug usage is primarily a matter of peer pressure, and usually this pressure is felt most strongly at the junior high school level. In high school, children are less amenable to peer pressure and more likely to develop their own values.

What about private schools? Private schools vary considerably more than public schools, and parents should evaluate private schools just as they would evaluate any outside professional service. They should look at the personnel involved, the history and tradition of the school, the degree of emphasis on learning and achievement, and measure how closely the social and moral values taught match those of the family. Because most teachers are trained in state universities and teachers' colleges, some private schools are moving in the direction of the public schools by introducing experimental programs. But the majority of private schools appear to be basically traditional and teach values in line with those of the middle-class family.

It is interesting that a large number of parents, especially fathers, are opposed to private schooling for their children. These parents often say they want their children exposed to all kinds of children, just as the parents were when they attended public school.

What these parents do not realize is that when they attended a public school in the 1940s and 1950s the value system taught in that school was rigidly middle class. Some children came from homes where there was considerably more or less wealth than the average, but the school subscribed to the middle-class values of hard work, achievement, competition, and respect for institutions. In fact, the value systems experienced in the 1950s public school were probably more "exclusive" than ones taught in today's private school.

One index of the type of values taught in the school is the child's cooperation with family values at home. Another index of a good school is the child's happiness. Children should be reasonably happy with their school and develop a sense of esprit de corps. One word of caution regarding private schools: Some private schools tend to pressure children excessively. If the child has only average intellectual ability or is somewhat below average, he or she may find the going very difficult indeed. There is no reason for a child to be studying two or three hours per night in the early grades, and a child will usually indicate his dissatisfaction directly or through fatigue, exhaustion, and physical complaints.

Should children have homework? Most children can benefit from homework after the second or third grade, but this should not be excessive unless the child is highly intelligent and self-motivated enough to spend long periods of time on homework. Many young children are proud to have homework because they realize their older brothers and sisters have homework.

Other Community Institutions

Other community institutions can also be very supportive and helpful to the child, or they can be destructive. Parents will need to evaluate agencies, institutions, and services just as they would evaluate professional consultation or the choice of a school. These institutions and services include churches, Scout troops, day camps, summer camps, community recreation centers, sports activities, and private and public services such as piano lessons, judo training, and art classes, to name just a few.

Any of these activities can add to the child's development or serve as a family-splitter in terms of values taught. For example, a community recreational center can provide an outlet for a child if it is well staffed by interested coaches and counselors. On the other hand, it can be an unsupervised area where drugs are available and where negative peer pressure is too frequently present.

It is generally acknowledged that recreation and sports are "good for kids." The reasons given are often vague, however, and usually relate to physical health and character building. While these are valid and important reasons, other specific values might be cited. Sports teach a philosophy that is truly American in spirit. Competition is the key word here, and sports teach self-reliance, endurance, and a striving for excellence. Some parents might see these as shallow platitudes and assume that their child gets a sufficient amount of these values in school and church.

As stated previously, however, this attitude of competition and excellence is being questioned in the schools more than most people realize. Some educators believe competition is harmful in any form and attempt to play down differences in student achievement. The modern report card, for example, often compares the child with only himself. This has merit in some cases, but teachers often find it difficult to know what each child is capable of performing, and the striving and achieving child finds little reward provided for performing at the top of the class. The authors feel that it is good for a child to compete against others. Perhaps the most important quality learned in sports is the child's attitude toward the outcome of the competitive event; that is, learning to be a "good sport"—win or lose.

A second area of importance in athletics is the realization that success in sports can contribute significantly to the child's self-esteem and in some cases go a long way toward correcting emotional problems. Many children who develop emotional problems and who would become involved in drugs or antisocial behavior have very low opinions of themselves because they have never really been successful in anything. Some children have suffered from poor coordination and will not be successful in the usual team sports. But the solution need not be to penalize the natural athlete by eliminating competition, but rather to find specific athletic areas where even less athletic children can succeed.

In some cases, planning for specific areas of athletic success for children in trouble may be more valuable than analyzing the child's problem areas. The children who do poorly in school or are ignored at home can often survive psychologically if they can reach the top in some athletic skill. This does not mean that parents should force their children into the organized sport of the parents' choice and then berate the child for lack of performance. If children are participating in areas where they have an opportunity for some success, they will learn the benefits of competition from their own performances and from a mature and well-meaning coach or instructor. If children are to become competent and mature adults, they cannot experience repeated failure or adult berating. This is as true of the nine-year-old child whose father wants him to be a homerun king, as it is of the nine-year-old student whose counselor wants him to run the school.

Dr. James Dobson, clinical psychologist, University of Southern California, states that parents mistakenly believe their love can insulate their child against various factors that reduce the child's self-esteem, such as unattractive appearance, quirks of temperament, intellectual limitations, or physical handicaps. He states that these parents are kidding themselves and wasting valuable time instead of evaluating the child's strengths and selecting a skill where the greatest possibilities of success lie.

Peers and the Community

It seems evident to the authors that peer influence has more impact upon children in the 1970s than ever before. This influence can be either positive or negative. On the positive side, for example, a good school will have a strong nucleus of healthy and achieving students who will provide leadership for other students in the school. This is of special concern to public schools in the

1970s, where the "brain drain" of bright middle-class students to private schools is hurting the public school. These students set the tempo not only for academic achievement but also for inter-personal relationships, morals, and manners.

The authors have also seen the negative side of peer influence and have been impressed for many years with the apparent effect of the peer culture on drug usage. The reason that mental-health workers have had limited success in helping children with drug problems is because even heavy drug-users are not necessarily mentally ill or emotionally disturbed. This is not to say that some drug-users do not have emotional problems or are not influenced by neglectful or emotionally disturbed parents.

In most cases, however, the drug scene can perhaps best be seen as a battle between positive and negative peer pressures. The negative peer culture is attractive to the child with low self-esteem and to the bored and sometimes lonely child, and serves as an alternative to the main stream culture. But it can also prove attractive to the relatively healthy and curious child as well as to children who have had difficulties surviving in the main stream. Children with specific learning disabilities, coordination problems, and various genetically based physical deficiencies are especially vulnerable to this subculture.

It is little wonder then that while mental-health workers have had limited success in probing the psychological mechanisms of children and their parents, programs that offer main stream cultural peer pressure are most successful in helping the chronic drug-abuser. They offer a meaningful alternative to the child who has been somewhat unsuccessful in the main stream or who has not received sufficient discipline and structure from family or community.

Drug programs located in Florida and other places achieve high rates of success through the use of positive peer pressure. These programs appear to achieve a balance between emotional confrontation and high standards of self-discipline. Rather than splitting the child off from the family, these successful programs are combining peer pressure with family pressure and a respect for American traditions and middle-class values.

This program has been accused of "brainwashing" because it definitely states right from wrong and because of the quick results it produces. Its critics probably believe that drug-abusers suffer from severe emotional problems learned in early childhood and from uncaring or neglectful parents. As a result, it is difficult for critics to see how positive changes can take place so quickly. They do not see the problem as a battle between competing subcultural peer groups. These critics may also see children as more mature than they are, and they cannot understand how these "mature" persons who are committed to lives of drug use can be changed so rapidly when they are treated realistically—as confused children with mixed loyalties to various groups.

Parents must be attuned to responsible studies and research of children in their area, and not the dramatic testimonials of individuals who have a vested interest in promoting drug problems. Unfortunately, some individuals who receive money to investigate and deal with drug problems are often biased, as their own livelihood depends upon developing the dramatic aspects of this problem and characterizing a minority of children as the more general population.

This is true, for example, of the issue of venereal disease, where some communities have attempted to place preventive programs in all elementary and middle schools. Yet the reported national incidence for all forms of venereal disease in the age ranges of zero to fourteen in 1973 was approximately 20 per 100,000. Even if this figure increases 400 percent, we are still at only 1 per 1,000.

Children are often not above manipulating their parents and emphasizing the drug and school problems of peers so that their parents will be more lenient with them. They play a game called "See Mother run" in which they describe these frightening aspects, with the child concluding "See what a good boy am I." Because such children state that they do not participate in these activities as do their peers, they then expect to have fewer responsibilities or more privileges. Of course, it may be that a particular child's peer group is engaged in these activities. It then behooves the parent to remove the child from this powerful and negative influence on his personality.

Parents may even have to consider moving their home from one residential area to another. Parents may have lived for some time in a residential area that has deteriorated and resulted in increased negative peer pressure.

When conditions are chaotic in the home and in the neighborhood, boarding schools should be considered as one possible temporary alternative. Usually the boarding school is not advisable until the child is fourteen or fifteen years of age. The parents should not be made to feel as though they are rejecting their child, and the child must be made to see that boarding school is not a punishment. The boarding school might be used for only one or two years in order to bring the child along in terms of the value systems of his peer group and to increase academic achievement. Parents need to be careful in their selection of a boarding school, with considerable investigation and great emphasis upon the character of the individuals operating the school and other criteria mentioned elsewhere in this book.

Many mental-health workers and child development experts still believe that if a child simply has many friends in his neighborhood and school, he is on the right track towards proper emotional development. This is no longer true in all cases. The major influence in some schools and some neighborhoods is tied into the drug culture and a general lowering of standards.

The authors have seen a number of healthy and bright youngsters who have been wise enough to limit their associations and friendships in the neighborhood as well as the school, much to the dismay of their parents and relatives, who would like them to become more popular. Even though the majority of middle-class youngsters still agree with middle-class values and traditions, the peer group can no longer be taken for granted, just as the public school can no longer be taken for granted as a supporter of family values.

Genes and the Community

Many times parents tend to overlook that both the seed and the soil are necessary ingredients in the child's development. While a child with average intellectual and physical characteristics may be primarily influenced by family and community, genetics can have an overriding importance in certain cases. This is discussed further in sections of this book relating to the learning-disabled child, the retarded child, and the gifted child. Children also differ markedly in their inherited temperament, physical ability, and size. These factors, along with differences in intelligence, are important in understanding the child's makeup.

Recent theories in the field of sociobiology indicate that there may be common behavioral patterns governed by the genes and shaped by evolution. A central theory of sociobiology is that the social behavior of individuals evolves to maximize the chances of genes like the individual's own to survive in the greatest number. This may indicate a stronger influence of genetics on social behavior than suspected previously.

While awareness of these genetic differences in the child's makeup is important, the parent should not necessarily attempt to create a genius or a professional athlete through concentrated and often faddish educational programs. Professionally administered intelligence tests are highly valid methods of determining the intellectual capacity of a middle-class child. The notion that all children come into this world on an equal intellectual footing and that through intensive environmental manipulation every child can become superior in intelligence is an absurd notion indeed.

The Child with a Learning Disability

What does "specific learning disability" mean? It's one of many terms used to describe a condition in a child that makes it very difficult for him or her to learn the basic skills of reading, arithmetic, writing, and spelling, even though the child has average or better than average intelligence. Many other terms are used, including developmental dyslexia, visual-motor perceptive disorder, minimal drain dysfunctioning, and congenital word blindness. In Britain, the official term is specific reading difficulty.

Initially, it was felt that these children suffered from brain damage because many of their problems were identical to those suffered by adults with brain injuries. Other research, however, has indicated that most of these children, unlike the brain-damaged person, largely outgrow their difficulty in adolescence or later. For this reason, many experts now use the term "maturational lag" in referring to this problem. Paul Satz, Ph.D., a neuropsychologist at the University of Florida, has done extensive research in this area and has identified a screening battery of tests to diagnose this condition prior to the first grade.

A learning disability may be defined as a lag in the maturation of the brain that delays differentially the development of those skills that are in primary ascendancy at different chronological ages. In other words, the brain's ability to learn in certain areas is not developed as quickly in learning-disabled children as in normal children. This delayed learning maturity is specific to each child and results in difficulties in the acquisition of the basic skills of reading, spelling, arithmetic, or writing. Research indicates this maturational lag affects as many as 10 percent of males and 2 percent of females. Unfortunately, since this condition has been labeled an immaturity of the central nervous system, some teachers will state that such a child is simply immature. While this is true in a sense, this type of immaturity is quite serious, and some studies indicate that more than 50 percent of juvenile delinquents, drug-abusers, and other children with various types of behavioral problems suffer from specific learning disabilities. While some children may eventually mature in terms of their brain and central nervous system, or eventually learn to compensate for the deficiency, they fall far behind in school and suffer great frustrations with resulting lowered self-esteem.

As pointed out by Lloyd J. Thompson, M.D., in the American Journal of Psychiatry, there are other analogous conditions, such as color blindness. According to Dr. Thompson, color blindness can be considered a developmental lag with an inherent biological basis. He reports that the newborn child has no color vision, and color blindness, like specific learning disability, "runs in families." As with learning disabilities, color blindness occurs in varying degrees and types, and about 8 percent of boys and less than 1 percent of girls suffer from this condition. As with learning disabilities, this condition is not related to environmental or emotional influences and the color-blind person may improve his color vision through appropriate training and practice. Dr. Thompson reports that evidence supports a hereditary predisposition in the specific learning disability.

All types of psychological problems can develop in the child with a specific learning disability and frequently this child will attempt to compensate for his feelings of inferiority by acting up in the classroom and perhaps taking on the facade of the "class clown." On the other side of the coin, a learning-disabled child may become depressed and withdrawn. A valuable book about learning disabilities for parents is the *Family Book about Minimal Brain Dysfunction* by Richard A. Gardner, M.D.

The following fictitious account of a learning-disabled-child may help us to better understand what such a child experiences.

Johnny is four and generally feels good about himself. He has fun playing games with his father and feels his mother is a warm person. Johnny feels secure about his home. He may have more trouble catching a ball than other children, or perhaps he doesn't always understand what his mother says to him. He may also experience some uneasiness. In kindergarten, he notices a puzzled look in his mother's eyes when she is talking with his teacher.

In first grade, Johnny is happy during his first two months in class because the teacher is warm, like his mother. He feels the teacher likes him, even though he doesn't "catch on" as well as some of the other children, he "prints backwards," and the teacher must tell him to sit still quite often. It is hard to sit still, though, especially when other children are moving and papers are rustling and the raindrops make such a loud noise on the windows. Later in first grade, the teacher becomes more stern and tells Johnny to try harder, but for Johnny it is very difficult. Johnny's parents ask him if he is happy and if he likes school and he answers yes. His parents begin to help him with his schoolwork and Johnny becomes anxious. What's wrong here? I wonder if I am stupid?

When summer comes, Johnny begins to feel better but has a twinge in his stomach when he remembers what school is like and that summer will not last forever. Now Johnny is in second grade and his new teacher seems to be starting out angry and tells Johnny that he could do the work if he would just try harder. Some of the other children ask Johnny what is wrong with him, and he hears the word "retard." Other children give him funny looks and giggle and wink when he cannot understand his work. He tries to hide his papers sometimes because there are so many red marks on them.

At home Johnny's father is becoming angry. There is no time to play with him because his father wants to "help" him with his work. Johnny is tired of work, however, and sometimes doesn't sleep at night because he is worried about school the next day. His sister, who is one year younger than Johnny, reads better than he does. He finds this makes his parents happy, and he isn't getting along with his sister as well as he used to. Johnny's parents have a meeting with the teacher, and Johnny discovers that he will fail second grade and that his sister will be in the same grade as he.

School is out again and Johnny is happy for a few days but then discovers he will attend summer school while the other children, including his sister, are out playing. Now Johnny is in the second grade again and his sister is in the same grade. She doesn't tease him but thinks he is "different." His father is very angry now and there is no time at all for games or fishing. Johnny's mother tries to make up for this and lets him get away with things at home. He doesn't want his mother to be extra nice though. He wants to be friends with his father like he used to be. The work is easier for a while in second grade because it is the same thing that he had before, but soon it becomes just as difficult as it was the year before. Johnny takes some tests with a nice lady who has him put blocks together, and he overhears his parents say that he has good intelligence. His father says that maybe he is lazy.

A lady asks him if there is anything wrong at home, and Johnny says he doesn't think so. He finds out he is not to be held back in second grade again and this makes him happy, but he realizes he will not be able to do the work in third grade. Johnny starts to wonder why grownups are doing this to him, and he decides that either they aren't very smart or they don't care about him.

Johnny is now in third grade and does not like school at all. He has stomachaches in the morning, but when he goes to the school clinic the lady tells him to be a big boy and that there is nothing wrong with him. His teacher tries to help him at first, but he has to miss art and recess so that she can give him extra help with his reading and spelling. He had thought he was pretty good in art but now he doesn't have even that. Some of the other kids pick on him, but he finds if he acts like a clown and cuts up in class the other children will laugh at him instead of calling him stupid. He finds the other children "like him" when he cuts up in class, and he'd rather be thought silly than stupid. He is sent to the principal's office for misbehavior and is told that he is only hurting himself and that there is no place in his school for a clown. A lady called the social worker talks with him in school and again he is asked if there is anything wrong at home. Now he is able to say that there are some things wrong. His father is mad at him, and he fights a lot with his sister. His parents hire a tutor to help him after school, but before long she is angry at him too.

Finally school is over and Johnny attends summer school again, but he is very tired in school and has difficulty understanding the material. In the fourth grade Johnny has more trouble in school, and his principal talks to his parents. His parents take him to the doctor, and he hears his doctor tell them there is nothing wrong with him physically and maybe he will outgrow it in time. Later his parents take him to a children's clinic, and he puts the blocks together again and goes every week to play in a room full of toys with three other boys. His parents also go to the clinic, and he feels a little better about getting along with his father and his sister. His mother does not let him get away with as much as she used to. He is still having troubles in school, though, and his mother takes him to the eye doctor. Again, he hears that there is nothing wrong and maybe he will outgrow it.

Johnny is now in the fifth grade. He did not fail because his parents tell him he would be too big to stay back again, but he still cannot do the work in school. At the end of the fifth grade he does fail again and now he is the biggest boy in his class. He learns he can push other children around if they tease him, and they had better not call him names, like "Stupid." Johnny finds some other friends who also act up in class and who have also failed in school.

He finds it is fun to skip school with his friends and see who can "rip off" things from the grocery store when the man is not looking.

Johnny is caught stealing and goes to Juvenile Court. A probation counselor asks him how he feels, and he tells him that his family is angry at him, that he feels stupid, that he hates school.

How can a parent determine if his child has a specific learning disability? The Developmental Checklist at the end of this section contains many characteristics of grade school children with this disorder. No child will have all of these signs and almost every child will have a few, but the child who appears bright in many ways and who is having great difficulty learning in school and who demonstrates many of these characteristics may very well suffer from a learning disability. Psychologists and educators working together are usually able to diagnose this condition upon referral from the family pediatrician.

What kind of evaluation can be expected in the diagnostic assessment of the child with a learning disability? The testing conducted by the psychologist and educator will consist of extensive individual tests of intelligence to estimate the child's approximate intellectual capacity. The child will also receive tests to determine where deficits exist that prevent intellectual capacity from being fully used. This testing will also include measurements of silent and oral reading comprehension, arithmetic computation and concepts, and written and oral spelling.

Some commonly used tests are the Wechsler Intelligence Scale for Children and the Stanford-Binet Intelligence Scale. These tests of intelligence are often used in conjunction with tests such as the Illinois Test of Psycholinguistic Abilities and various achievement tests. The use of direct observation and checklists can help to offset the cultural bias involved in the usual standardized tests and to take into account factors such as fatigue, medication, the use of lenses, and other factors that might lower the validity of formal tests. The Developmental Checklist at the end of this section can be used either by teachers or parents to record observations of the learning-disabled child's behavior and can be mailed in by the professional for a computer-assisted printout that may provide a guide for further diagnostic investigation and possible corrective steps.

Many other specific tests measuring neuropsychological development are selected by the psychologist for use, depending upon the child's age and individual circumstances.

The vast majority of children are not embarrassed or frustrated to any extent when they take these tests. Many parents fear the child will attach some stigma to this evaluation, but most children see it as further academic testing of the type they receive in school. In addition, most of these children have already concluded that they are really disturbed or stupid and that, fortunately, no one has yet discovered this. They are greatly relieved when this problem is identified, labeled, and plans are made to remedy it.

The primary treatment for learning disabilities is called "remediation." It should be conducted only by a sensitive, highly trained, and experienced educator who has demonstrated proficiency in the area of specific learning disabilities. Remediation can take place two or three hours per week on a one-to-one basis with the learning specialist or in small groups twice a week, or even for an entire day. The specialist can help parents decide what schedule is best for their child.

Children requiring the one-to-one remedial work are often those who are very young and unable to tolerate the stimulation of a group setting or those who need constant emotional support and reassurance. The full-day setting is not necessarily reserved for the most severely deficient child, but for the child who is in a school that has high expectations for its students or that overstimulates them through lack of discipline or structure, as in the open space classroom. Such children need to be removed from that stimulation altogether so that they can be relieved of the frustrations and pressures that will prevent them from overcoming their problems. There is presently a trend in public schools to handle special problems of this type within the child's regular classroom, and while this is an admirable goal, it is idealistic and unproven at the present time. Most teachers do not have the time or the skill to properly help a learning-disabled child, and many classroom settings continue to expose such a child to excessive pressure, peer ridicule, and overstimulation.

There are some cautions in order here. Parents are strongly advised *not* to seek help from a retired teacher or other regular teacher who may have good intentions but who does not have the highly specific skills necessary to help a learning-disabled child. While proper treatment is expensive and will usually take from one to two years, it is certainly a reasonable expenditure when compared with other expenses such as orthodontia and the increasing costs of a college education. It seems to the authors that it is better to give the child the opportunity to realize intellectual potential and to avoid unnecessary emotional and physical stresses, even if the large expenditure now means that the child will have to work his way through college later. Statements made in Chapter 11 regarding the skills and credentials of a specialist working with a child certainly pertain here also.

A further caution relates to the special class or school for the child with learning disabilities. Sometimes these facilities purport to work with children with learning disabilities, but upon closer examnation the parent will find the school also offers services for retarded children, children with severe brain dysfunctioning, hyperactive children, and children with serious behavioral problems. These classes, whether public or private, can teach the child to misbehave in a very direct fashion. The analogy to what happens to a young public offender who ends up in jail and learns to become a criminal may apply.

Besides remediation from a learning specialist, what other assistance may be necessary for the learning-disabled child? While a learning disability is not caused by the environment or the family, it serves to place a magnifying lens over all of the typical problems found in any family. Therefore, counseling may be necessary to help both the child and the parents cope with this condition. Siblings must be stopped from "lording it over" their brother or sister who suffers from a learning disability. Some of these children have problems with large motor coordination, and fathers must learn to hide their feelings of disappointment and engage their children in areas where they can be successful despite a lack of coordination. Such activities might include swimming, riflery, fishing, and camping.

Parents must avoid attempting to "cure" learning disabilities themselves, since it invariably leads to a loss of patience and to lowered self-esteem on the part of the child. A learning-disabled child, more than most, needs a positive relationship with parents, who should not deal with this weak area except to occasionally help the child when requested. If the child is spending long hours with homework despite the school's statements that they understand the condition, parents must not hesitate to extricate their child from this very damaging situation by discussing the problem with the school again or even removing the child and placing him in another school.

What actually takes place in remediation? The skilled clinician or teacher in the learning-disability classroom will attempt to teach the child through his strong and open avenues of learning while at the same time remediating the weak and underdeveloped areas. For example, a child may be able to learn well visually but may have trouble understanding oral directions and experience great difficulties in writing down what he or she knows. This child would be taught to learn through the strong, visual avenue and at the same time carefully and patiently taught to improve skills in the weak auditory and visual-motor areas. Sometimes large motor coordination exercises are helpful, and while the "patterning" approach to correct brain dysfunctioning has not proved beneficial, this should not be confused with large motor exercises that teach the child such spatial concepts as left-right and up-down. These ideas will help the child identify the written letter and differentiate between letters that are similar in appearance such as p and q, and d and b. The evidence regarding the validity of gross motor exercises is incomplete, but they may benefit learning when properly applied by learning specialists. The authors do not believe that most speech and hearing clinicians and developmental optometrists have the full range of background and experience to diagnose and remediate the learning disability problem.

Medication may also be helpful in the treatment of the learning-disabled child and the parent should, of course, consult with a pediatrician regarding this possibility. Such medication is essential for some children not only to reduce activity level but also to increase concentration and memory.

Parents will sometimes place their learning-disabled child in a private school in the hope that he or she will receive more individualized attention because of the small teacher-class ratio. This can backfire, however, because ordinarily expectations for achievement are higher in private schools than in public schools. Parents may need to consider placing a child in a public or private school where less pressure exists while the child receives extensive and sometimes fatiguing remedial help. After the child has been fully remediated, he or she may then benefit greatly from small class placement where he or she can receive more attention and greater pressure to achieve.

If the learning-disabled child remains in a public school either temporarily while receiving remediation or permanently, it is usually necessary to ensure that the child is not exposed to the open space or "pod" concept. Learning-disabled children need a great deal of structure and less visual and auditory stimulation than other children. While many children are assigned to a certain school either on a geographical basis or as part of the implementation of integration, many school boards will allow a child to transfer from one public school to another if they are made aware of the learning disability problem and the environmental difficulties presented by the open space concept.

Some parents have made effective use of the so-called free school for a temporary placement for their child to receive intensive remedial work. Most free schools follow a humanistic philosophy and do not place a high emphasis on the basic skills of reading, spelling, and arithmetic. While this has serious disadvantages in the long run, most learning-disabled children enjoy this type of placement because there is little academic pressure. A "free school" can be effective if used on a selective and temporary basis while the child receives professional treatment for the learning disability.

Even after the learning disability has been largely remediated, there may be residual effects, and parents will need to be selective in the curricula to which their children are exposed in junior high and high school. Children who suffer from auditory weaknesses should delay taking foreign languages, especially if an oral teaching approach is taken rather than a written or reading one. These children may also have problems in courses where lengthy note-taking is required. Often it is advisable to teach typing to the learning-disabled child, especially if he or she has a weakness in writing speed.

An awareness on the parents' part of subtle residuals can make a great difference in the child's progress. This is why the learning disability problem is so frustrating and elusive to the child, teacher, and parent. For example, children with auditory weaknesses may be doing fairly well with a foreign language taught through a literary approach. When they change schools they may have great difficulty with the same foreign language because it is taught through an oral approach. Another child who has a weakness in visual-motor skills may do well in a social studies course in which there is a great deal of class discussion and do poorly in a science course that requires extensive note-taking in class. Once the parents recognize the particular weak avenues in their child, they will tend to study the child's curriculum more by process than by subject matter content alone.

The learning-disabled child who has average or below average intellectual ability may be best placed in a public school where low average groupings are available. Even after the learning disability has been remediated, such children may benefit from a comprehensive junior high school where vocational programs are utilized or from a work-study program in which they can seek employment while taking a minimal load of academic subjects. Most school systems offer vocational training at approximately the age of sixteen—some offer it for younger students—and in Florida, for example, some learning-disabled children are eligible for remedial help and vocational guidance through the State Department of Vocational Rehabilitation at the age of sixteen.

The Developmental Checklist

1. Seems happier and experiences fewer problems during summer and/or weekends than when in school.
2. Usually cannot say the days of the week or months of the year in correct order.

3. Reverses or transposes letters or numbers when writing. For example: "dog" becomes "bog"; "cat" becomes "tac."
4. Has trouble catching a ball (size of grapefruit or smaller).
5. Can write well if tries but usually doesn't try.
6. Child's father or mother never did that well in school, failed a grade, or did better in high school or college than in third through eighth grades.
7. Cannot pronounce the sounds of certain letters.
8. Has trouble organizing written work and seems "scatter-brained" or confused.
9. The child is the class clown in a nonmalicious way.
10. Uses both hands for same activities. (For example, he or she sometimes eats with the left hand, sometimes with the right.)
11. Does well in almost everything but school.
12. Mother or father had problems knowing left from right or was clumsy as a child.
13. Says he (or she) does not want to go to school or does not like school.
14. Reverses or transposes letters or numbers when reading.
15. Reading is below grade level or child is in a low reading group in class, but does better in mathematics.
16. Would rather print than write.
17. Confuses left and right or cannot tell left hand from right hand without stopping to think.
18. Clumsy or somewhat below average in baseball, football, kickball, jump rope, or skipping, although may be able to swim well.
19. Has trouble remembering three or more consecutive directions.
20. Can read fairly well orally but has trouble comprehending the meaning of written words.
21. Seems bright in many ways but does poorly in several school subjects.
22. Has trouble concentrating, frequently shifts from one activity to another.
23. Seems to "forget" physical complaints when school is out for the summer.
24. Has trouble expressing his thoughts clearly or gets things in the wrong sequence in his speech.
25. Complains of feeling sick on school nights or in the morning before school (two times per month or more).
26. Has trouble with time concepts, confusing today, tomorrow,

and yesterday; trouble counting how many days from Tuesday until Friday, for example.

27. Handwriting described as sloppy or careless.
28. Frequently turns wrong way when told to turn left or right.
29. Teacher says child is slow to finish work (doesn't apply self, daydreams a lot, or falls asleep in class).
30. Has trouble understanding written or oral directions.
31. Impulsive, does things on spur of moment without thinking.
32. Lacked clearly understandable conversational speech by age of three and one-half.
33. Does much better on multiple-choice tests than when required to write spelling words or answers.
34. Cannot tell time.
35. Teachers feel child works far below ability level.
36. Seems to learn much better when being helped individually than in groups.
37. Can memorize a spelling list perfectly and still fail a test on the same words the next day or a few days later.
38. Difficulty with arithmetic (for example: cannot determine what numbers follow eight or sixteen; may begin to add in the middle of a subtraction problem.)
39. Temper tantrums.
40. Lies about school, grades, and homework.
41. When sent to find something, child often cannot, even though it is "right there."
42. Problems in speech development.
43. Is a hard worker when doing something he or she likes and when it is not related to school.
44. Can tell time only by the quarter hour.
45. Great difficulty learning the sounds of letters.
46. Loses place more than once while reading out loud for one minute.
47. Cannot tie shoes or only with great difficulty and sometimes needs help.
48. Teacher says child can do better if he or she really tries.
49. Great inconsistency in academic work from day to day or even hour to hour.
50. Appears immature; seems somewhat younger than his or her age.
51. Overly talkative, interrupts, "motor mouth."

The Hyperactive Child

Hyperactivity may affect as many as 5 percent of school-age children, and its most demonstrable characteristic is excessive activity, often from infancy. Many of these children can be identified in early infancy and have feeding problems, colic, and sleep problems. The hyperactive child appears to be born with his "motor running at sixty miles per hour" and he can be insatiably curious and very destructive. Some mothers of hyperactive children are fatigued to the point of exhaustion. Often, they receive little support in their attempts to cope with their hyperactive child because of the bias among many child specialists to blame parents for almost all problems children exhibit.

As such children enter school activity may lessen gradually but they often cannot sit still in class and are easily distracted. They will notice the sounds of pages turning in the classroom and noises that are barely discernable to people equipped with normal powers of concentration. In Little League baseball, such children may be watching the birds fly by as the ball is hit past them. Interestingly enough, a large percentage of these children can concentrate when watching a favorite television program or in their physician's waiting room. Many of these children could best be described as hyper-*reactive*; that is, extremely sensitive to the stimulation of groups, such as in the classroom, and to any situation in which a great deal of extraneous stimulation is present. Less professional descriptions include phrases such as "ants in the pants" and "motor mouth." Most young children are active and distractible, but when this behavior becomes extreme, the problem is hyperactivity.

In addition to the dominant characteristic of hyperactivity itself, many of these children are less demonstrative in terms of affection and suffer from poor coordination and learning problems similar to those of the learning-disabled child.

Like the learning-disabled child, hyperactive children naturally experience strained relationships with their parents, teachers, and peers, but fortunately, they tend to outgrow this condition of hyperactivity, as does the learning-disabled child.

The treatment of the hyperactive child is primarily a medical one. Unfortunately, some of these children are seen by psychotherapists who place them in a play therapy room filled with toys. It is little wonder that progress is very slow. Certainly it is important to understand the hyperactive child's feelings, just as it is important to recognize any child's feelings, but the first rule of work with hyperactive children is to set up a firm and structured situation for the child.

The pediatrician will often prescribe medication for the hyperactive child that usually takes the form of a stimulant drug. Such a drug has the paradoxical effect of reducing activity and distractibility and increasing attention span. These medications are not sedatives that are "poured in on top of children" to control them, but they appear instead to be a necessary replacement for immature brain function.

Research has indicated that children receiving medication for hyperactivity are not in fact less active even though they appear to be so, but that their activity becomes properly channeled so that they are able to concentrate normally. Medication simply allows the hyperactive child to function at a more normal level until the brain matures on its own. Therefore, when maturation takes place in adolescence, the medication is no longer needed and is withdrawn. Many parents are reluctant to place their child on medication of this nature because they fear their child may become addicted. Studies have indicated that hyperactive children who are medicated with stimulants have shown no sign of addiction or other abnormal bodily functions.

In many cases, parents are able to tolerate their child's high activity at home, but medication is necessary during the school hours if the child is to have an opportunity to learn. In these cases, medication is usually taken early in the morning and again at approximately 11:00 A.M. Unfortunately, some schools are unwilling to dispense medication, and the children are not old enough to do it themselves. In such situations, one early morning dosage is better than none at all. If these children are receiving remedial learning help during the summer, they typically also need their medication approximately one half hour before their remedial work. Once again, the pediatrician is the key person to treat this problem and to make recommendations if deemed necessary.

Upon referral from the child's pediatrician, a clinical psychologist may be in a position to help determine the degree of hyperactivity and to advise the parents regarding appropriate structure in the home.

Many of the disciplinary procedures outlined in Chapter 4 are especially helpful to parents with a hyperactive child. It is extremely important for the parents to place hyperactive children in a room where they can "cool off" when they are having temper tantrums or behaving in a destructive and uncontrollable manner. Many parents are unable to follow through on this procedure and as a result, the child rules the home in a tyrannical manner. While the child may give in at times, he or she knows that if pushed far enough parents will give in since they are not ultimately and finally in control of the situation.

When such children are having tantrums or behaving destructively, parents should take them calmly by the arm and without any expression of distress or disgust, lead them to their rooms and close the door. The child can be removed a few minutes after the tirade stops. The child should not be placed in the room for a set period of time because the length of stay should terminate when the child calms. Many parents will respond, "He just kicks the door, destroys objects in his room, or simply comes out of the room." In this case, the parents may have to lock the door and teach the child gradually that it is a privilege for them to place him or her in the room without locking the door. The parents may need to remove objects that the child might destroy in the room and gradually replace them as the child shows increasing self-control. Some parents feel such children will hurt themselves physically by banging their heads against the floor or wall. Injury rarely occurs, but this type of concern should be checked with a physician.

This type of response to temper tantrums may be an essential starting point for the child to learn that parents can control the child's behavior effectively. Once the child knows this, then the parents can work outward from the enclosed room with the child knowing that further problems may result in being returned to the room. For example, the child can be required to sit in a chair facing the wall after a tantrum with the knowledge that if the child does not sit in the chair he or she will be returned to the room. Later the parent can advise the child to stop the tantrum or the child will have to sit in the chair. The verbal admonition to self-control will thus be linked to the chair and ultimately to time in the child's room.

Some hyperactive children also suffer from learning disabilities or from such marginal concentration that even on medication they have difficulty learning in the classroom. These children need to be in a classroom with little stimulation and perhaps even carrels or enclosed areas that further remove them from such distractions as movement and traffic flow. Because these children are so active, many teachers make the mistake of giving them excessive recess and recreational time. In many hyperactive children, this only results in their becoming so wound up that they are unable to perform for thirty minutes to an hour after recess. Such children will often benefit from quieter activities within the school rather than unchecked activities on the playground.

The Intellectually Slow Child

The mildly or educably retarded child has an intelligence quotient, or I.Q., that falls roughly in the range of 50 to 75. An I.Q. of 100 is average. With luck and proper instruction, the mildly retarded child will be able to live independently in the community as an adult and upon completion of all of his schooling should rank between the fifth and seventh grades as a student.

The authors believe it is important for parents to have their mildly retarded child evaluated extensively by a private psychologist, who is licensed by a state board of examiners, for several reasons. In a small percentage of cases, the child may be suffering from a serious emotional problem that pulls test scores down to the retarded range, and this child may in fact have average or better intellectual capacity. In other cases, a child may be suffering from a severe learning disability so that extreme deficits in one area are pulling down overall average intelligence scores. Other children may be suffering from brain dysfunctioning, which reduces the overall average intellectual score on a standard intelligence test. Granted, this represents only a small percentage of children who are classified as mildly retarded, and the authors do not suggest that parents take their child from one qualified professional to another over a period of time with the hope that one will discover the child is not actually retarded.

Properly administered and interpreted intelligence tests are highly valid and reliable despite recent criticisms of this testing by some psychologists and educators. Actually, the criticisms should be leveled at those inexperienced and untrained examiners who are now administering intelligence tests and misusing the results, rather than at the tests themselves. A medical analogy would be the performance of appendectomies by inexperienced and untrained people. If this occurred, appendectomies would come under similar criticism because these partially trained individuals would undoubtedly cause more problems than they would solve. (Controversy exists about the racial bias of intelligence testing when used for educational placement and classification. For white middle- to upper-middle-class children, the tests are valid.)

The child can be evaluated by a qualified professional as early as the age of four to rule *out* retardation, although it is difficult to rule *in* retardation before the age of six or seven. If the child has had two evaluations after the age of six at a two or three year interval, and retardation is clearly established according to testing, then further testing to determine retardation is of dubious value. Additional testing may be helpful, however, to determine a child's achievement level and may be necessary to set up an educational or remedial program for the child. Approximately 50 percent of the retarded children seen by the authors are functioning below their achievement abilities and can benefit from specialized learning techniques without undue stress. Many of these children have not learned the basic learning skills they will need in the marketplace because they have "tuned out" their teachers in special classes and schools.

Parents will need to take a close look at the individuals (not just different programs) who work with their retarded child. A loving and dedicated staff committed to helping the child reach his maximum potential is a key ingredient in helping the retarded child.

The authors have found that many procedures utilized in the special educational training of learning-disabled children can be employed successfully with retarded children. Most retarded children will have some areas of ability that exceed other areas and can be taught through their strong avenues of learning. This teaching does not seek to raise the child's I.Q. but to help realize potential. To make his way in an increasingly sophisticated world in the 1980s, the mildly retarded child will need to reach at least a fifth grade level in reading comprehension and arithmetic computation. These complexities are seen in the use of credit cards, charge accounts, and checking accounts, to name just a few. The mildly retarded child is also often eligible for services through a department of vocational rehabilitation or similar state agency at age sixteen.

In terms of general ability and thinking, mildly retarded children will fall two or more years below their chronological age in ability when they are six through eight years of age and three or four years below their chronological age when they are nine, ten, or eleven. They usually remain at the mental or thinking age of ten or eleven as an adult.

Moderately retarded children have I.Q.s betweeen 25 and 50, and they need support, care, and help as they live in the community. They can benefit from work in a sheltered workshop and will need to be in the custody and care of an adult. The severely retarded child falls in an I.Q. range of approximately 5 to 25 and may require institutional care. Unfortunately, most state institutions for the severely retarded are greatly lacking in facilities, staff, and professionalism, and a great deal of work remains to be done in this area.

The Gifted Child

Gifted children are truly uniquely endowed individuals. Such a child's I.Q. of 140 or more on an individual I.Q. test performed or supervised by a licensed psychologist makes him or her one in many hundred. One of the major concerns for parents of such a child is that the child might become bored in school and present anxiety or behavioral difficulties. Another fear is that the child will learn to quiet curiosity and questioning because he/she may threaten classmates and teachers.

Middle-class gifted children will usually survive best in a school with high academic standards, although they many need to skip a grade. Many people feel the gifted child should not skip a grade because this may produce problems in high school in dating, driving, and athletics. There is no perfect solution, but often the truly gifted child will fit in better with students who are one year older in terms of social and athletic endeavors as well as academic pursuits.

Some public schools are offering programs for gifted children, and parents will need to take a close look at their own public school programs before agreeing to allow their child to participate. Some of these programs consist of taking the child away from the regular classroom for a few hours a week of stimulating discussion. This may help to keep this child's curiosity alive, but it may also make the child even more aware of the dullness of the regular school curriculum. Because the child spends much time in the regular classroom, it appears obvious that this is where the major input must be made.

Some of these ancillary programs appear to offer the child a dose of humanism in disguise. The child is taught to clarify values in his life and is encouraged to question institutions and authority figures. What educators as well as parents must remember is that the gifted child is a *child* and not an adult in a child's body. This child's obvious intelligence can result in parents and teachers giving excessive responsibilities, especially in terms of decision-making, which can result in a great deal of anxiety. While the gifted child needs intellectual stimulation commensurate with a high mental age, he or she needs a great deal of structure and security as do all children. While a gifted child at the age of six may be able to accomplish academic tasks as well as an average child who is eight years and four months of age, this gifted child may operate socially as a seven-year-old and should certainly not be treated like an eight-year-old.

Occasionally, the gifted child will have some developmental skills that are only commensurate with chronological age. For example, the gifted six-year-old may have the reasoning, comprehension, and abstract thinking abilities of an eight-and-one-half-year-old but the writing skills of only a five-year-old. In this case, the child may need to spend part of the time in school with higher grade levels in such subjects as reading but return to a first or second grade group for writing instruction. This child may also need remedial help to close the gap between the high intellectual capacity and present functional ability, which has been reduced by a lag in some developmental skill such as writing.

The parent of a gifted child might have to seek assistance for the child away from the school. Gifted children may become bored by school, even though the school is offering all it can. Special courses after school can be organized to provide the child with educational challenges.

3 Principles and Mistakes

This chapter developed from the practical applications later illustrated in Chapters 4 through 8 and from the professional experience of the authors.

Nine Key Principles

More than a part-time job

Parents must dedicate themselves to child-rearing as a responsibility and obligation of procreation. No one ever said child-rearing was easy. It demands a great deal of unselfish commitment and the belief that it represents one of the highest values of life.

It is usually difficult for the unmarried person or the married person without children to understand the values, rewards, and continuity in life provided by children in a dedicated and loving family. The excitement, adventure, reward—and even the personal growth of the parent—must be experienced to be believed.

While the rewards of parenthood are many and equalled only by the husband-wife relationship, these rewards must be earned. It is difficult, if not impossible, to become a successful businessman, physician, teacher, or even hobbyist without expending a great deal of energy and time. This is certainly even more true in parenting.

It is quite difficult for the mother, who usually spends more time with the children than the father does, to hold a full-time job and still care properly for her children, especially if they are younger than ten. Part-time work after a child is five and placed in a full-day kindergarten program is possible, but again can be an energy drain.

The decision for a mother of young children to work should be made jointly by the parents, who should consider whether work produces tension or calm in the family and whether it allows adequate time for child-rearing.

It is also quite difficult for the father, who is usually the primary income-earner, to work a sixty- or seventy-hour week and still provide his share of the parenting for the children and support for his wife. He should be prepared to delay, postpone—and, in some cases, even give up—advancement in his business career just as the mother may have to postpone her career objectives.

If the father is not prepared to work at child-rearing, then he should not complain at a later time when he does not "know" his child and when his child models himself after others. Some fathers will attempt to use their profession or business as an excuse for not being available to the family, but a closer look will usually show that they could reduce their workloads, especially attendance at functions that are ego-builders and not mandatory for the well-being of his customer, client, or patient. In some cases the wife will accept such a rationalization either out of naïveté or because she may wish to have the children all to herself.

It is important for parents to be available to children because it is difficult to *program* quiet time, conversation time, and other meaningful relationships, especially before the child is eight or nine.

It is impossible for parents to know when their children will have problems or feel a strong need to communicate. This does not mean that parents must be at the "beck and call" of their children, but, on the other hand, it is most difficult to set up arbitrary times for communication—especially with younger children. They have not learned to postpone gratification and may, with time, forget what they wanted in the first place.

Children cannot be foisted off onto parent substitutes for the major part of the parenting work. Such substitutes include relatives, child development specialists provided in some day-care and nursery projects, schools, summer camps, and other institutions that exist to provide *partial* substitute parenting.

Raising a child might be compared to owning a business. No one will take quite the interest in a business that the owner does. Similarly, few "child-care workers" and teachers will take quite the interest in children that their parents do.

The competent child-care specialist may be able to offer consultation. Because specialists are not emotionally involved, they may have more objectivity in assessing family patterns and interactions.

Child-rearing really boils down to the life values of the parents. If parenting and family life have significance to you in terms of a reason for existence, then the parenting will usually be of a high quality. If you worship other "golden calves," such as materialism or success, then a child will suffer.

Many child-rearing tips and tricks are ways of helping marginally dedicated parents to control their children while freeing the parents for "more valued pursuits."

Children, not China

The second key principle helps to clarify the first. While the first principle states that a real commitment to parenting is necessary, the second principle states that this does not mean parents should become overly involved in developing their child's "psyche." Neither does it mean that children are highly fragile and intricate organisms who can only be raised by the professional child development expert.

Edward Zeigler, former Director of the Office of Child Development, United States Department of Health, Education, and Welfare, presented this view in an article appearing in the September 1973 issue of *Human Behavior*. Dr. Zeigler stated that "many parents view their young child as more fragile than he or she really is." He went on to say that "even the very young child is a relatively tough, active, structuring human being with a personal capacity for growth that almost guarantees a normal course of development provided the child is protected from physical harm and is given the love and care of ordinary devoted parents."

Zeigler noted that parents often walk about their homes as if on egg shells and do not enjoy their children's development. He cautioned against early developmental and intellectual "tricks" that are intended to raise the child's I.Q. or guarantee his healthy development. There are games and books that can be purchased that offer promises of increased I.Q. for a child, and these should be avoided.

Based upon our experience with relatively normal children, the authors view the child as somewhat analogous to a train on a track. Parents may need to remove obstacles from that track and prevent the train from becoming sidetracked or derailed, but they should not attempt to construct the train, which is already sturdy and on a well-defined course.

There are exceptions to this, of course, and occasionally a train becomes equipped with some damaged or undeveloped parts, such as a child with a learning disability who cannot read. This requires speedy repairs with professional assistance. The main point is that the child—like the train—usually comes pretty well built and does not need to be remade, though each may need inspection occasionally to ensure proper development and protection from obstacles on the track.

We do not believe the normal child needs to "learn" to be curious or to communicate. He or she is born with curiosity and an urge to communciate. A poor school may provide an obstacle to the normal development of the intellect; however, an overly concerned parent might also provide an obstacle to the developing autonomy of the child. A disturbed peer group may sidetrack social development.

The comparison of a child to a train is, of course, a weak analogy, as is any definition of a child. For one thing, unlike a train, the child is constantly changing and growing as he or she goes along his or her "track." Another important exception to the analogy is the area of values. While you should not attempt to force-feed educational toys on the child, especially at an early age, it is extremely important to teach the child a set of moral and ethical values. Parents *are* obligated to provide values so that their children can make constructive choices later on. These values have to do with the *"whys,"* not the *"whats"* and are taught in the home through example, in the church or synagogue, and via appropriate community resources such as Scouting, YMCA, YWCA, and others.

Unfortunately, there are professionals who take the opposite view. They feel that parents should experiment with their own children in terms of intellectual and personality development, usually based upon theories derived from clinical situations. At the same time, these experts encourage the parents not to impart their values to the child.

Family-breakers

"Family-breakers" can be defined, in general, as factors, forces, or elements that prevent or interfere with family communications and family cohesiveness.

Frequently, textbooks and the popular press cite poverty, hunger, ghettos, and mobility as causes of family breakups. With the possible exception of mobility, it is unlikely that the middle-class reader of this book directly experiences any of these issues as family-breakers.

Middle-class family-breakers are more subtle and more insidious. By recognizing these factors, parents can attempt to steer their children through the community environment more successfully.

Some of the family-breakers are obvious, however: Father working too much, mother in too many civic clubs or employed for too many hours, friends and neighbors being too dominant in the flow of the family.

One subtle family-breaker is the television set. The process of watching television requires that people face away from each other and toward an electronic box. If no attempt is made by family members to communicate with each other during a television program, values can be acquired by the children that are out of parental control.

Another subtle family-breaker can be the children's peers, if they do not share a parent's values and do not participate in activities that the parent sees as valuable. Yet another family-

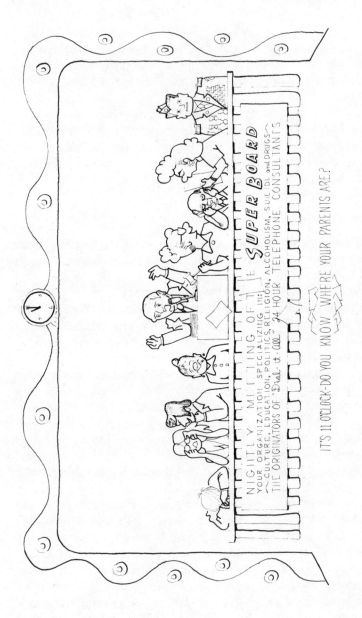

70

breaker is the general intent of the statement "do your own thing." This statement can suggest irresponsibility toward oneself and toward others.

Much reference has been made in this book to the importance of a parent's obligation to the child; however, the child certainly has a reciprocal obligation to his or her parents. The child who "does his own thing" may easily reject the notion of responsibility toward parents or the rest of the family.

Certain philosophies and programs in our public schools can also work to divide families. Bussing children to schools that are not in the children's neighborhoods frequently results in parents not knowing their children's peers and being totally unable to exercise control over these important influences on their family.

Frequently, a school counselor or school psychologist speaks to a child and neglects to speak to the parents. There is often an attempt to keep information confidential from parents to protect the school's counselor-student relationship.

Unfortunately, parents rarely exercise control over whether their children are to be seen by a counselor and even more rarely exercise control over who that counselor is to be. The counselor's reputation credentials, intentions, and techniques are often unknown to the parent. In an area so vital to us as our beloved children, significant decisions are being made that frequently exclude us.

A family-breaker of major and far-reaching significance is the recent interest and activation of birth control, venereal disease protection, and abortion advice clinics. In our opinion, it seems clear that when a child is receiving confidential information concerning these issues, major and destructive things are being done to our families.

The great majority of middle-class parents we have counseled do not want their children to be sexually active during early and mid-teenage years.

In this regard, Dr. Blaine Porter, dean of the College of Family Living at Brigham Young University and the past president of the National Council on Family Relations, reported in a May 8, 1973, Public Broadcasting System presentation as follows:

"I believe that the family should have the primary responsibility, [of sexual education], not a government agency. We have failed to talk about some of the other alternatives that are available; and one of them, I believe, would be to help the teenagers to be less sexually active. I know of thousands of teenagers in this country who are not participating in premarital sex relations. And do you know, it is interesting that not one of them has a problem with venereal disease, an unwanted pregnancy, an abortion, or getting birth control information."

The authors believe that chances are quite good that teenage children may receive sex, abortion, and contraception information through a public health department or public school and that (1) they have no need of it, (2) it will take place without the parents' knowledge, (3) it might lower the children's values, and (4) it may alienate them from their families.

"Crisis-seeker" is the term we have coined to identify those usually well-meaning individuals who may split families because of their desire to eliminate some social problem. Crisis-seekers seem to follow a similar pattern in their work. First, they identify a crisis that relates to a minority of the population, and then they attempt to have a law passed or programs introduced that will not only affect that small percentage but also the rest of us, often with an overall lowering of standards and values.

An example of crisis-seeking is the proposal to permit and encourage birth control counseling for minors without the consent of their parents. While illegitimacy affects only 1 percent of the female American teenage population—and an even smaller percentage of middle-class children—crisis-seekers would like to pass a law that excludes parents from these crucial decisions regarding their own children and lowers values generally.

A recent specific case is seen in a position paper compiled in Florida, to support sex education in the public schools. This paper was presented to a county school board in March 1977. The paper reported that in 1976, in Pinellas County, Florida, there were 465 births to girls seventeen years of age and younger, including one eleven-year-old. Approximately 73 percent or 340 of these births, were out of wedlock. Alarming statistics? Yes, indeed. But further analysis reveals this total of 340 births represents only 1 percent of females in all the middle and high schools of the county.

After analysis such as this, one must question the "epidemic" proportions of these 340 out-of-wedlock births. Certainly, everyone would like to solve the problem of illegitimacy. However, when efforts are made to contact 100 percent of the children with information that pertains to 1 percent of the population, we are dealing with crisis-seeking. Further, it is the authors' opinion that when issues such as illegitimacy and birth control are presented to children in public schools—particularly without parental involvement or input—the values being taught in schools are reduced.

Another example was an effort to start a venereal disease education program in the public schools. While an extremely small percentage of students suffered from venereal disease, this problem was proclaimed to be of epidemic proportions and the goal was to have V. D. posters in every classroom. Some of these posters seemed to make light of sexual relations, and the general message of the program was "how to protect yourself from venereal disease *when* you have sexual relations" (authors' italics).

Anchors

Children need an anchor. Children must have some feeling of organization at home as an anchor to hold onto as they continue the rapid development that affects them physically, socially, and emotionally. Regular mealtimes, bedtimes, homework times, and free times all contribute to a sense of stability and structure needed by the child.

Because young children are evolving, changing, and growing, they need a considerable amount of structure outside of themselves to develop a positive self-image and feelings of continuity. If the family environment is unstable and disorganized, then children can easily develop anxiety and fearfulness or become quite inhibited as they attempt to provide themselves with some form of structure.

While the need to provide structure and continuity for the ever-changing and developing child seems obvious to most parents, many experts are pressuring parents to reduce structure and stability within the home. We see many parents who tell us that counselors and school officials uniformly give advice to reduce structure, and the humanistic literature is replete with admonitions of the dangers of structure. The experts define this structure as "rigidity" and feel it will inhibit the child's "creativity and growth." "Rigidity" may be a pseudonym for "values," however, and it appears logical that family values would come under attack by groups that would rather have families adopt *their* values, which, by the way, they define as nonvalues.

It is not only the very young child who needs a feeling of order in the home. As children continue to grow, rapid changes take place within them during the adolescent years, and the need for stability does not subside.

The need for structure and anchors in the home has become even greater in recent years. With rapid social changes, social experimentation, and conflicting values now being taught in community institutions and the media, a sense of structure and continuity is even more important in the home. The structure of the home, then, rather than inhibiting children, can give them a sense of mastery over changes within themselves and changes in society.

As a result of this mastery and the security it provides, children can become spontaneous and creative and can use their energies in productive ways rather than having them drained off by the anxieties resulting from the internal and external shock waves of rapid change. If "anchored" by dependable parental values, children can make constructive use of the changes within themselves and within their society.

Children change

This is the developmental principle. It is surprising how frequently adults forget that children vary from adults in one overriding way: their constantly changing development.

A child is a changing, unfolding human organism, and children at various ages in the same family cannot be treated in exactly the same way. Many parents are apparently attempting to be "fair" with their children, but what they are actually doing is attempting to make children at different ages feel that almost everything can be worked out to everyone's satisfaction.

Children of different ages should not be given the same responsibilities and privileges. Older siblings should have more responsibilities and privileges, and younger siblings should have fewer.

While this may not seem fair to some parents, it really is the only approximation of justice possible. This is an obvious but easily forgotten principle, and some parents do discipline all their children in exactly the same manner, even though there are widely varying age differences. Their children all have the same bedtime, receive the same allowance, or have the same type and number of responsibilities, as though age differences did not exist. Some parents fear that younger siblings will resent older siblings with a slightly later bedtime, for example, and that the younger children will not feel that they are equal to the older siblings.

In fact, younger children are not equal to older children in many respects, and they will find this same type situation when they enter the "real world."

The authors have seen problems develop when younger siblings have been encouraged to feel they are socially, intellectually, and physically older than their age level. Such encouragement can make the younger children feel uncomfortable because they recognize at some level that they are unable to handle the privileges and responsibilities given by the parent, and they may lose some of the safety and structure inherent in the child's role. Meanwhile, the older siblings often see their parents's attempts at fairness to be unfair. We are reminded of the parents who permitted their seven-year-old to watch a television special until 11:00 P.M., three hours past his bedtime, because they believed he could learn something. By eleven o'clock, the seven-year-old was exhausted, irritable, and no longer watching the television; his fourteen-year-old sister was angry at him for disrupting her viewing and angry at her parents for permitting him to stay up. The parents were angry at both of the children who destroyed their evening because of their behavior.

Accentuate the positive

This advice might sound like a cliché, but it represents an entire philosophy of child-rearing and human relationships in general.

The positive approach is in opposition to the crisis-seeking approach. As the problem-solving formula indicates in Chapter 9, one of the first approaches is to ignore the problem and work on the positive aspects of the child's behavior.

The authors have seen many cases in which parents present a problem and naturally expect us, as professionals, to invest ourselves heavily in discussions and to recommend solutions for the specific problem. While this is sometimes an effective approach, it can be dangerous because it can blind us to the child's positive traits and skills, and we can begin to see the child only in a negative light.

In many cases, we have helped parents and children overcome a specific problem by setting it aside for the moment and working on the positive vocational, recreational, academic, and behavioral aspects of the child. This, in turn, has often resulted in increasing the child's self-esteem. The problem behavior has then disappeared.

Such a situation is similar to a medical one in which an individual who is somewhat run-down physically may be susceptible to colds, viruses, and other physical ills. These problems can be treated medically as they occur, or the individual can be helped to develop a more positive physical condition that will resist these stresses on its own.

This approach has sometimes been called the "therapy of success" and relates to William James' definition of self-esteem as the amount of convergence between aspirations and achievements. While children may feel more comfortable if they lower their aspirations to a more realistic level, they can also feel greater self-esteem by increasing achievement in some area in which they are capable.

The authors believe it is extremely important for the child to have feelings of success and achievement in some areas. If parents and counselors focus on unfulfilled aspirations in one area of the child's life, they may forget or negate achievements or potential achievements in other areas. The child may then feel that he or she can do nothing right.

An example of this is the six-year-old girl who cannot jump rope in the neighborhood because her physical coordination is poor. Instead of putting all of our energies into helping her to jump rope better, we could introduce her to other sports in which she might excel, such as swimming, and enhance her self-esteem there. Another example is the nine-year-old boy who fights a great deal with his more academically successful eight-year-old brother. In addition to attempting to deal with that situation, the parents should keep in mind that a little more individual father-son time working on a strong area of interest and ability for the nine-year-old will go a long way toward diluting the sibling rivalry.

Some parents complain that they cannot find "one single thing" that a child does well. This only means the parent is taking for granted a great deal of positive behavior. When one looks at the number of activities in which a child participates during a given day, it is apparent that the majority of the behaviors taking place are positive. There should never be a case when it is impossible to "catch a child when he is good."

It is a myth that praise spoils a child. Rather, it is a lack of discipline and of responsibilities that will spoil a child—not praise. Properly timed praise is essential for the development of pride and positive self-esteem.

Parents sometimes ask why some professional psychologists and other counselors deal only with specific crisis problems within the individual and ignore the overall individual and the many environmental situations in which human beings find themselves. This specialization may have developed because some theorists believe a child is fragile at an early age, somehow becomes indestructible later, and, therefore, must face up to and conquer any situation encountered. These professionals become crisis-solvers rather than becoming more broadly concerned with the individual.

The analogy of the train may again be useful. These specialists seem to feel the train needs to be constructed completely during the first six or seven years of life. It can then remove obstacles from the track all by itself. It is our impression, however, that environmental obstacles can develop all the way along the track, even into adulthood, and in many cases it is important to remove such negative situations from the child and to concern ourselves with building the child's self-esteem and feelings of success.

Another reason for popularity of the crisis approach among professional counselors is the belief that parent-child interactions totally influence the attributes the child carries into adulthood. With increasing encroachment by outside parenting agencies who take the crisis approach and the rise in alternative value systems, parents today, unfortunately, no longer maintain the same overriding influence they once did. The crisis-seekers attempt to solve parent-child problems to which they may have contributed.

Absence of democracy is not a dictatorship

The family is not a democracy, even though some people have the idea that it should be. The analogy between a family and a

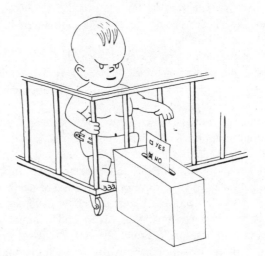

political democracy is not a good one. The political democracy is comprised of individuals who have a fully developed intellectual capacity and who are legally responsible for themselves. If they do not agree with the decisions of that democracy, they are free to leave. Children are not free to leave their families. In addition, members of a family are much more closely linked than the varied and sometimes widely separated members of a democracy.

Even though children certainly have feelings, they do not have the developed intellectual ability or social and interpersonal experience that their parents do.

It is important for parents to look at their children's feelings and reason when possible so that decisions that are ultimately made by parents can provide a learning experience for children. This does not mean, however, that children can cast equal votes on major decisions involving the entire family or even, in some cases, regarding themselves individually.

The authors have seen a few cases of families run by "non-benevolent dictators" who set extremely high expectations for their children and give no real indication of affection for them. These kinds of parent-child relationships which lack love or affection can certainly produce emotional and behavioral problems. This "dictator" approach in some families, which implies that children are not to be heard or seen, is often represented by the "ultrahumanist" as a typical picture of American families. In the groups and social class we have worked with, however, this type of family makes up an extremely small percentage.

The ultrahumanist and democratic position is seen more frequently and appears to be having an unfortunate influence on many families. These families are often swayed by psychological and sociological researchers who report that the democratic family is the healthiest and most productive. The researchers' definition of "health and productivity," however, often excludes reality.

The authors have seen many problems develop from the position of unequivocal democracy within the family. Some parents have become afraid to make decisions or provide necessary structure for their children. They have lowered their expectations so that the child has no desire to excel or achieve. Because they believe their children should not be exposed to frustration of any type, some parents are afraid to discipline their children. Yet, because they set few standards and rarely discipline, these same parents are forced, out of their love for their children, to be extremely watchful and give their children less freedom than is found in most families. As a result, the children lack independence and self-reliance and become anxious and confused because of the lack of structure in their lives.

It has been our experience that the "democratic" parent often ends up screaming at or punishing a child because of the lack of overall structure and discipline in the family. If this does not occur in the middle years, then certainly in adolescence there is a last attempt by such a parent to come around to a more structured and responsible type of family situation, but at that late date it only further provokes the child who is used to freedom and a voice in family decisions. A frequent result is the attitude of the parent who says, "I have tried everything and now I give up."

The humanist-democratic school often promotes reasoning with children in every situation, regardless of developmental level, in the belief that children will grow as a result of experience. This group seems to believe that whatever a child does has a reason behind it and that the child can learn and, with discussion, benefit from what he or she has done. Some theorists think that all behavior is a function of experience that has been incorporated into the self-concept and the particular situation of the moment. They seem to believe that children can change behavior when they see that their values and expectations "mesh."

They recommend this approach regardless of whether the child is two or eighteen. This single-mindedness may stem from their belief that human beings are entirely unique and blessed with many godlike qualities. People are seen as competent, knowledgeable, and able to empathize with others. Despite this belief, humanists generally regard authoritarian, opinionated, or structured parents as the primary obstacles to the development of their children. The child is viewed as a developing human being with unlimited potential, while the parent is viewed as a representative of a possibly inhibiting institution: the traditional family.

Parents are criticized for their attempts to lead, control, or set expectations for their children. The humanist advice appears to be contradictory, however. On the one hand the child is seen as a self-developing, self-fulfilling human to whom parents can only be a bother. On the other hand, parents are expected to help their children understand their emotions. Children must never experience confused feelings, according to this school of thought, and it is up to parents to help their children sort out their feelings so that they will continue to grow normally.

The humanist sees democratic parents not only allowing their children to develop values and expectations but also loving their children more, respecting them more as individuals, controlling them less, and being more open and honest in communications.

The authors have seen many parents who have attempted degrees and variations of this simplistic approach, and many difficulties result. Often children cannot recognize and reason regarding their behavior because they do not have the intellectual capacity or judgment to do so. This, of course, varies according to the child's age. Other factors besides the present situation and the child's self-concept are important in influencing his or her behavior.

Some children cannot change because of brain dysfunctioning so that values and expectations cannot "mesh" unless the parents understand the specific condition of a child. At other times, children do not realize the causes and components of behavior because they simply do not listen to their parents or because the parents have difficulties communicating with the children.

At times parents may want a behavior pattern to continue because it rewards them in some way (the naughty but "cute" child, for example). At other times, children as well as adults are victims of habit and cannot bring reasons for their behavior into consciousness. They operate in somewhat irrational ways or are influenced by habit patterns that cannot be changed through discussion. Parents also encounter dangerous situations, such as a small child wanting to play in the street, in which there is no time for lengthy discussions.

Humanists honestly believe they are the friends of the children, but when they attack parents as a primary obstacle to a child's development and when they attack the family through unsupported views that the nuclear or conjugal family of father, mother, and child is finished, then they are hurting the child.

It has been our impression that the majority of parents love their children more than some social scientists realize, seeing their children as real people in a real world and accept them for what they are. They do not attempt to manipulate them through subtle communication techniques that are narrow and basically dishonest.

These parents do present values to their children, and they should. Such values give children a foundation on which to base their own value system at a later time. Humanists often see themselves controlling their children to a lesser degree than the average parent. But in fact they are often subtly manipulating their children to their point of view, and they are selling a value system no more or no less than the middle-class family. The real question has to do with which values are being taught, how they are being taught, and their effect on the child.

As to the issue of control, we have found it to be much more beneficial to the child for a parent to control the child openly rather than covertly. A parent should set standards and controls on the outside, take a stand, and allow the child to openly and honestly express agreement or disagreement with the values presented.

Fortunately, the "democratic" approach takes too much time for individuals and families in the real world to implement. It also requires a great deal of skill, so that most parents give up on attempting to practice this form of "psychotherapy" with their own children.

Learning is natural

Motivation to learn is inborn. Children are naturally curious. Motivation to learn, like hunger, is a need the child must satisfy.

If a child is unable to learn, then the question is not to teach the child how to learn but rather to discover what is interfering with this natural developmental process. Obstacles might include maturational lag in the central nervous system, poor schooling, or other factors.

Parents sometimes say their child is lazy and does not want to learn, whereas in almost all cases it is a matter of discovering which obstacles have made learning unenjoyable and, therefore, have reduced the natural motivation to learn.

A child will naturally want to do that which is interesting, rewarding, and maintains his or her self-esteem in the classroom. A child will naturally want to do well in the classroom, but if unable to perform may put up a facade of carelessness or even become the "class clown."

While curiosity is inborn and does not require enhancement, this does not mean that a child will be motivated to perform every type of behavior the parent wishes. For example, there is usually not much curiosity associated with emptying the garbage each day. Yet this may be a reasonable parental request, depending upon the child's age. In this case, some added privileges may be given to the child to acknowledge increased family responsibilities.

Different Strokes for Little Folks

Children are different from each other because of their genetic makeup. This important fact can be easily overlooked, however, perhaps because of the influence of some popular writings that claim that the parent is entirely responsible for molding the child.

Children vary in their basic temperamental outlooks and can often be identified at a very early age as active or calm. Children vary in their intellectual capacities, their physical and athletic abilities, and even their susceptibility to physical and emotional problems. This is not to say that children should be allowed to go their own ways without parents teaching them responsibilities and values. But parents' expectations for their children should vary according to a child's capabilities. The parents must be aware of their child's strengths and weaknesses so that outlets for the strong capabilities can be found and weaknesses can be remediated when necessary.

It is a mistake, for example, for parents to expect that two brothers are capable of "A" and "B" work in school when one has superior intellectual ability, is physically and socially more mature than his classmates, and suffers from no known physical problems, and the other is smaller than his peers, is less intelligent, suffers from allergies, and has coordination problems that affect his handwriting. Most parents are aware of the many differences among their children, but sometimes their observations fall on deaf ears when they seek professional help. They may even be accused of spoiling or pushing the child who suffers from subtle deficits.

Children also vary in their personalities. Some children are sensitive, thoughtful, and easily hurt emotionally. Such children can often be dealt with best in a quiet, thoughtful way. Outgoing and boisterous children may respond to lighter and more humorous approaches. The quiet child should be respected as much as the more open and sociable child.

Nine Key Disciplinary Mistakes

When an hour is more

Parents often do not realize that children experience time in longer intervals than do adults, and parents occasionally use time intervals that are too long for rewarding or punishing their children.

For example, a parent might say to a child, "If your grades are up this year, then you can use your driver's license." A year is too long a period for such a punishment, and it would be much more appropriate to tell the child that if he or she accomplishes a certain amount of work each evening, then the car will be available for an appropriate period of time that evening.

Similarly, parents will "ground" their children, requiring them to stay at home except for school attendance for six weeks or more. Such a restriction loses its impact because it extends over such a long period of time. The child will give up attempting to achieve the required goal because the privileges have been taken away for so long. It does not make sense to the child to work hard when the privileges will not be reinstated until what seems like the "distant future."

Children need parents more than institutions

Parents will occasionally fall into the "crisis-seekers" trap, either through a need to build their own egos or a bona fide commitment to help the community. As a result, they may spend too much time in community activities helping other people, and other people's children, during a period when their own children need them for the consistency and interest necessary for a stable self-concept. Evening time at home with the children is especially important when they are younger than ten.

When a spade isn't a spade

Parents tend to reason excessively with their children when the children are young, especially when they are younger than nine or ten, and then parents often do not reason with the children when they are adolescents. Just the reverse of this should be practiced.

Many parents reason unsuccessfully with their young children. When the children are older and want to reason things out, and are more capable of doing so, the parents are ready to institute the types of controls and discipline that were more appropriate—and often lacking—earlier.

This appears to be an area in which some of the popular human growth movements have gone astray. They found their approaches to be somewhat effective with overly intellectualized university professors and graduate students and enjoyed some success with college students and adolescents. Some of the humanists then insisted on rigidly applying their philosophy to young children. As a result, some of these children are not receiving proper structure and security because of the concept of the "fully democratic family."

Many parents treat their children as though they are adults, either through excessive reasoning or through shouting matches that develop into games of "tug-of-war." The child then may feel more adult than he or she is and, therefore, more responsible. This can result in a great amount of anxiety and guilt for the child.

This does not mean that parents should not attempt to understand their children's feelings. (For examples of how to understand a child's feelings see Haim Ginott's classic book, *Between Parent and Child*.)

To understand and reflect a child's feelings, however, is not to reason extensively. Most parents in the middle-class population of the United States who have been exposed to brief seminars in communications and emotional facilitation apply what they have learned in the form of excessive reasoning. Such an approach does not appear to be the intent of the humanist movement, and perhaps these parents were highly intellectual though unaware of their feelings in the first place and thus were drawn to humanist seminars. Perhaps their exposure to this approach was too limited for them to alter themselves, and it appears that they have only memorized and programmed verbal expression of feelings.

Even though parents understand and reflect how a child feels, they should not disregard "behavioral consequence" as a form of discipline. For example, a parent might say to a nine-year-old child: "I know you are real mad at your sister and you would like to call her names, but if you call her that again, you are going to your room." Notice here the combination of a recognition of feelings, imposition of discipline, and a lack of confusing language. A humanist might simply say: "I know you are real mad at your sister and would like to call her names. I understand."

Loud isn't strong

Parents sometimes threaten when they should listen to children express their feelings and show that the feelings are understood. Then parents can take some action. Parental threats remind children that parents are aware of an indiscretion and will most probably take action at some later point. Threats lose their power if overused, however, and some parents who consider themselves to be tough disciplinarians because they scream, threaten, and yell are actually inconsistent and even "soft" disciplinarians.

They lack any type of disciplinary structure, and as a result, these parents lose control over their emotions and their children. Many children are able to calculate the number of threats and warnings from a particular parent before that parent will take action and will normally respond only after drawing the maximum number. This can be an interesting game for children who are bored or angry at their parents, but it is rather hard on the parents' nerves.

Double trouble

Misbehavior that results from discipline must be disciplined.

Children will be disciplined and, often, because they do not like the punishment, will violate some other rule that is then unfortunately ignored by the parent. For example, if a brother has been abusive to his sister at dinner and is told to go to his room for ten minutes, he might "accidentally" bump his sister on the way. Parents might ignore this misbehavior, but it really is a crucial time for additional discipline. If the new infraction is ignored, then the original discipline has been displaced, and a new game has started in which the child is the winner.

Remember, children may desire to win these "games," but in the vast majority of cases they are much less happy when they do win, even though they do not realize why.

Work before play

There is an adage: "work before play." For example, if children are requested to empty the garbage as a daily chore, they may sometimes reply that they are going to have ice cream first and will empty the garbage afterward.

Work should come before play, and whenever possible children should be asked to accomplish assigned tasks before play or pleasure. This sequence provides a reward for work—a model that characterizes many child and adult situations.

Spanking isn't always punishment

Parents should not continue to use a punitive measure if it is not helping to bring a child's behavior under control. Results from a new punishment may not occur immediately, however. A child may test a new disciplinary measure, and behavior may become worse before it becomes better. But to use a punishment over and over when there are no discernable results over a period of time is obviously not beneficial to the child or to the parents. Punishment that could be physically harmful to the child should never be used.

Children should not be humiliated in front of siblings, peers, or classmates as a method of punishment. Repeated humiliation can harm a child's self-concept, even though he or she might respond occasionally with the correct behavior.

The authors see spanking as one of several parental responses to misbehavior that can be used with a child, and like other responses, it will vary in its effectiveness. Spanking can, on the positive side, indicate concern, interest, love, and consistency. As with other disciplinary measures, if used inappropriately, in too great a degree, or at the wrong time, it can indicate rejection and abuse. Spanking after the age of nine or ten is rarely useful.

Not little adults

Parents should keep their expectations in line with the child's competencies and remember that a child *is* a child and not an adult. When we have seen problems with expectations, harm occurs most frequently when parents demand too much of a child.

Parents must remember that children are not "little adults," and if they want their children to become superathletes or superscientists, they must realize that this will occur when the children are adults and not before. Children are dependent and require the opportunity to grow into adulthood with the feeling of protection and security.

Even the father who wants his son to be a "he-man" should remember that his child will not be a he-man as an adult unless he is protected, taken care of, made to feel secure, and yes, even babied occasionally as a child.

If a boy is forced into a role of a he-man as a young child, he may grow up to be a man who is physically strong but who is anxious, insecure, frightened, and possibly passive beneath his he-man facade.

Thou shalt not lie—if you're an adult

Parents should trust their children and be aware that lying and exaggerating are normal and even frequent throughout early childhood.

Parents should accept what is believable and not hesitate to check on what is incredible. We have seen many parents who are able to tolerate the immaturities of their children in most areas but who become extremely upset when their young children lie to them. Lying, of course, should not be ignored. Young children should be instructed calmly to tell the truth.

Young children cannot always be truthful just as they cannot always tie their shoelaces. They are learning about life and need to be taught. It is important for parents to determine how a child got into such a bind that lying seemed to be the only way out and then to offer the child alternative solutions. If children continue to lie for no apparent reason, then in all likelihood they are doing it to seek attention.

In this case, parents must look at other areas in the child's life where they may be forgetting to react positively. Fantasy-filled "tall tales" in children under the age of six are not harmful yet should not be encouraged, because to do so is to add to their credibility.

The idea of trust must be based on responsible behavior by the child as well as by the parent. However, if the parents of a sixteen-year-old boy suspect that he's taking drugs, for example, they may have to search his room with or without his knowledge. There has been a betrayal of trust by the child, and of course, the parents in this situation are trying to protect their child from serious harm.

4 Guidelines for Problem-Solving

The formulas in this chapter can be used by parents who have identified behavior problems in their children that need to be changed. These suggestions work well in conjunction with ideas presented in Chapters 6 through 10. This chapter presents several useful ideas but is not intended to substitute for professional consultation.

Children Sometimes Solve Problems Too

When a behavior problem develops, the first step is to discuss it when both parent and child are calm and the child is not misbehaving. If children are able to suggest a cause for their problems, and even more important, a reasonable solution or partial solution, then their ideas should be tried. Even if parents suspect that a child's solution is not realistic, it may be worthwhile to try it to determine if it is feasible and to indicate to the child that they are willing to work with him or her against this "foreign" problem. Such cooperation should not extend to levels of absurdity, however.

The possibility of a child providing workable solutions to behavior problems is more likely after the age of nine and much less likely before the age of six.

Parents should avoid lectures and lengthy reasoning sessions with their children. Pretend that each word exchanged is worth one dollar and try not to give $300 in exchange for $5. Long answers by parents to short questions by children can produce many problems but few solutions.

Of course, a parent and child, especially an adolescent, might spend many hours discussing various topics at one sitting if they are so inclined. But usually these lengthy talks, in order to be constructive, are not precipitated by a specific problem the child is experiencing. And ideally, they are not attempts to identify as a problem something that the child does not believe is a problem.

Situations Change

It is important that parents be acquainted with the particular fears, anxieties, and changes coming from within a child at various ages. (See chapters 6 through 10.)

It is also important for parents to think about a child's relationship to his community and peers. Try to think of the events in the community or in the home that might have changed before the onset of a problem. If a child has experienced a problem in the past, is there some incident or change in his or her life now that also accompanied this problem in the past? Has school just started or ended? Has one of the parents been preoccupied with a project and away from home more than usual? Has a relative come to visit or someone in the family left the household on a trip? Has a new program been introduced at school or a change made in the method of teaching?

Input from Others

Sometimes persons outside of the immediate situation can see patterns of behavior and problems more clearly and may thus provide useful advice. These other people might include peers, siblings, teachers (religious school and regular school), and relatives. These people can be very involved with your children and see them quite differently. One is reminded of the parent whose child is complimented by a teacher and replies: "You can't be talking about my child!" because at home the child has been difficult for months.

Roadblocks

Parents should review Chapters 2 and 3 to attempt to remove any "roadblocks" that may be creating the problem. Roadblocks may include such issues as allowance and bedtimes, individual time with the child, the child's performance (including school achievement and recreational and athletic endeavors), and peer influence.

Is the child functioning at the appropriate grade level or above in all subjects without an excessive amount of study? Is the child's ego being built up through recreational, vocational, or athletic activities? What about the allowance situation? Is the family providing an anchor for the child, including daily schedule, mealtimes, relaxation times, and protection from excessive activities? Are you as a parent following the basic keys to development as outlined in Chapter 3, and are you free of the common mistakes and myths of child-rearing as delineated in Chapters 3 and 10?

In most cases, parents will find the answers to their children's problems in these areas. A child's poor performance in school or a hectic family life-style can cause behavior problems.

When Ignorance Might Be Bliss

If the problem still exists and parents have honestly and courageously examined and removed roadblocks in the family and environment, the next step is to *ignore* the behavior unless it is physically dangerous to the child or to family members, or destructive to property. Simultaneously, parents must make a special effort to recognize the child's positive behavior and to comment on and reward it while ignoring negative behavior. Sometimes a child may be misbehaving because he or she is rewarded by parental response to negative behavior. When parents stop their negative response and ignore bad behavior, it may disappear. The cooperation of members of the immediate family, other relatives, teachers, and other significant people in the child's life is important so that they will not continue to reward negative behavior.

Be Specific

To ignore a negative behavior and recognize positive behaviors, it is necessary to pinpoint what the negative behavior is and somehow keep track of its increasing or decreasing rate of occurrence. Pinpointing is an extremely important step because if parents are not exactly sure what behavior they object to, then it is going to be very difficult to change that behavior or keep track of whether improvement occurs.

Parents will often have a vague impression about some attitude or behavior they would like to change. They might state that their child has the "wrong attitude about things" or "lacks respect or drive." These generalities are convenient ways of expressing a problem, but they need to be broken down into specific *behavioral* objectives.

For example, does the disrespectful child say things that indicate he is disrespectful? If so, *who* does he say them to, *when* does he say them, and *how often* does he say them? If a parent says that a child does not keep his room straightened, does this mean that all of the clothing in the child's room should be picked up from the floor and placed on the back of a chair and that the bed should be loosely made? Or does it mean that all clothing should be hung properly in the closet and the bed perfectly made? Or, does it mean something between these two extremes?

Pinpointing a specific *behavior* is very important and often parents will find that after they have pinpointed a specific problem it either disappears or was not the problem they had initially thought it to be.

Frequently, parents will feel confused and helpless when advised to specify a child's inappropriate behavior. "Good heavens, there are a dozen things I would like to change!" they say. Although it is true that the child may be involved in a number of negative behaviors, it is important that the parents pick out one behavior that they feel to be meaningful (not necessarily the worst one) and to approach it before going on to others.

Ogden Lindsley has done much of the pioneering work for this approach, and he has used the expression "first things first, one at a time" to characterize it. If parents take one problem at a time, their success in solving it will often help a child solve other problems.

Any one of the problem behaviors exhibited by a child may symbolize a power struggle in the home. Helping the child to overcome a particular difficulty in a reasonable way and without a sense of crushing defeat will provide the child with structure and security. It is impossible to change several behaviors at one time, and the attempt only dilutes the parents' energy and problem-solving skills. By resolving one problem area, the parents may be able to break a "tug-of-war" that characterizes their particular parent-child relationship.

In addition to allowing you to have a starting place, pinpointing is important for another reason. Through pinpointing, you can become more objective and avoid expecting the impossible from a child. You can keep from becoming exasperated and criticizing your child in sarcastic and dehumanizing ways.

Keep a Record

For a child to benefit from the parental approach of ignoring negative behavior and rewarding positive behavior, a record must be kept so that improvement—or the lack of it—can be measured. Without some record of the frequency of negative behavior, parents might be inclined to give up this approach when in actuality the rate is gradually declining. It is not necessary to write a narrative of the negative behavior but simply to put marks on a piece of paper, checks on a chart, poker chips into a glass jar—any way to note each time the negative behavior occurs.

By recording or ignoring negative behavior, parents will sometimes cause the behavior to diminish greatly or stop. A reduction indicates that the child has been receiving some "hidden payoff" or reward through attention, even if negative, for the behavior, and that the recording has given the parent some other way of responding. This change in parent response might also indicate to the child that the parent is taking some adult, consistent, and organized steps to help him correct his behavior.

The payoff may involve several members of the family at one time. For example, a little girl may provoke her older brother into hitting her because she likes to get him into trouble and the comfort she receives from her mother when she becomes slightly hysterical. Her older brother may be happy to oblige her with a blow because he likes to see his little sister put on a show and his mother aggravated, knowing full well she will not discipline him but only raise her voice with repeated threats. It is even possible that the mother in this situation might be rewarded by feeling needed. She might also want to bring her husband more into the family interaction, and these incidents will give her some crisis to present to him for his solution. Naturally, these participants would not be aware of their own payoffs in such situations.

What next?

If the problem behavior persists, the next approach involves taking a more direct attempt to correct it. In order to do this, it is first necessary to determine whether the problem relates to something the child fears or whether it relates to a lack of appropriate behavior (such as a refusal to carry out responsibilities) or a behavior that is annoying or harmful to others.

Fear

If parents are dealing with a fear, then they should use "positive association" and introduce "gradual practice" to make the child feel less afraid.

Positive association is made by introducing people or objects that are familiar and comfortable and that inspire security in the child. These comfortable associations are introduced into the fear situation to dilute it and then are gradually withdrawn as the child becomes more comfortable. For example, if a child is afraid to use the toilet alone, the parent might need to stay nearby and gradually withdraw as the child becomes more comfortable. Favorite toys or a favorite blanket or a fun object that evokes a positive emotional response incompatible with fear could also be introduced into the situation.

Gradual practice means to take many small steps to allow the child to gradually become accustomed to a frightening situation. The child who is fearful of school, for example, might be taken there during nonschool hours to get used to it without the distraction of regular school activities. A very shy child might be encouraged to answer the telephone at home or smile and say hello to people he sees during the day. Gradual practice can also take place through fantasy and role-playing. By pretending to experience the frightening situation, such as a bad dream, the parents may be able to give the child quiet reassurance while he or she re-enacts it.

In addition to using positive association and gradual practice to help frightened children, parents should also reward children when they show increased ability to tolerate or function in fearful situations or overcome their fears.

And pinpointing and recording (as covered previously) must be supplemented with rewards from parents when a child performs positively. Parents are often puzzled about possible positive consequences and sometimes feel that nothing is positive or rewarding to the child. They may come to this conclusion because their child does not become greatly excited with a reward. But the parents themselves are in the best position to observe those activities, social encounters, material rewards, foods, responsibilities, privileges, and other factors that children choose on their own.

The timing of these positive consequences will be unique to the child, and the parent will often be in an even better position to know what is rewarding to his child than will the child. For one child a positive consequence might be a story at bedtime and for another it might be the opportunity to dig holes in the backyard.

Sometimes a child's behavior resulting from fear can be a clue to a positive consequence. For example, if a child expresses fear about going to bed, keeps getting up for drinks, wants the light on, or in other ways resists going to bed, the reward of a drink before bed or the light on every other or every third night for nonfearful bedtime behavior on other nights might be the solution.

In conclusion, then, in the case of fearfulness on the child's part, it may be helpful to introduce positive association, gradual practice, and positive reward for successes.

Misbehavior

When a child is not carrying out responsibilities or is disobeying parents or is engaging in other negative behavior, the solutions do not involve gradual practice or positive association. Parents should pinpoint and record the behavior and then introduce negative consequences for negative behavior and positive consequences for positive behavior.

It is in this area that a closer look must be taken at the "payoff" that the child is receiving and that better timed and focused rewards for the child's positive behavior must be introduced. Parents must give positive consequences as soon as possible after positive behavior and must be consistent. It is important to be as consistent with a *new* consequence, whether it be negative or positive, as the child was consistent in evoking the *old* rewarding consequence. If a child provoked his or her parents's anger to irritate them and they responded each time inappropriately with rage then they were being very consistent. It is now important for the parents to consistently provide the appropriate response.

Two other principles may be helpful in eliminating negative behavior. These are "incompatible response" and "negative practice."

Because most children cannot concentrate on two things at once, it is sometimes effective to teach a child a positive response that occurs at the same time as the child's undesirable negative response, thus eliminating the negative response. This is "incompatible response." For example, parents might teach a child to practice good manners rather than punishing the child for bad manners. In this way the bad habit is broken and the child learns a positive habit at the same time.

"Negative practice" sometimes helps a child to bring a negative habit into awareness by consciously practicing the negative habit. For example, if a child does a great deal of thumb-sucking and appears to be unaware of it, often it is helpful if the child will consciously practice thumb-sucking in front of a mirror for a few minutes several times each day so that the habit will be brought into conscious awareness. This approach is not used to shame or humiliate the child but to enable the child to become aware of the sensations, reflexes, and responses involved in thumb-sucking or other negative behavior that is performed unconsciously. Once this awareness has increased, then rewards can be introduced to help eliminate the thumb-sucking.

Occasionally parents will make the consequences too extreme or delay them to the point where they are not effective. For example, taking away bicycle privileges for six weeks or a semester until grades improve is too delayed and too severe. It is much better to restrict use of the bicycle each evening when homework has not been done or, from the positive point of view, to offer the privilege of taking out the bike when daily responsibilities—including homework—have been accomplished.

Two other cautions are in order here. The first is that when new consequences are introduced by parents, a child will often test the change and things may get worse initially. This resistance does not mean the child is spiteful but that he or she is looking for consistency, structure, and control. Because the child has been responsible for setting these up in the past, change will be resisted. Once this change has taken place, the child will usually appreciate the safety of the control and structure provided by the parents.

A second caution is never exert excessive pressure on a child by instituting a system that allows no alternative, that is crushing to the child's ego, or that is embarrassing, even though it might satisfy the parents's specific goal. An example of such a poor punishment would be restricting a child to his or her room each evening for poor grades until they improve. The improvement will take weeks, and the child will miss desired social contacts or sporting events during that time. Both the child and the parents might see one or more of these events as beneficial or important. Examples of more moderate approaches are given in chapters 5 through 9.

5 The Behavior Checklist

In this chapter we present a checklist that can help children be more successful in the family. We do not recommend that the checklist be used for all children or by all families, but if behavior problems occur, this list is frequently a rapid and relatively unobtrusive way to alter a child's behavior.

If a child is performing responsibilities reasonably well (and remember we should never expect perfection from a growing child just as we do not from a grown adult), if no behavior problems of significance are present, if parents are able to reward their children for good behavior by thanking, complimenting, and spending positive time with them, then, of course, the checklist may not be necessary. Also, it is not necessary to keep a chart forever. This approach can be helpful for one or two months until a greater degree of responsibility, structure, and positive reward is developed.

The behavior checklist is a technique that can help a child assume responsibilities and chores more willingly. It also adds additional structure and external control to a child's day, thus aiding the growth of self-control. It can help a child become more cooperative. It helps make clear the expectations that parents have regarding their children's behavior and activities both inside and outside the home. It can remind parents not to expect more from their children than they are capable of.

The checklist itself should be posted in a central point in the home such as on the refrigerator or near the dinner table. Parents should not single out one child with whom to use the chart. All children between ages three and fifteen should have separate charts if this technique is used. (Sample checklists of representative behavior in different age ranges are presented in subsequent sections of this chapter.)

A check, point, or star should be placed in each box for the accomplishment of the prescribed behavior. They can be exchanged for rewards, such as ice cream or special candy. Or they can be exchanged for desired activities, such as a special movie or a trip to an amusement park. To give such a "grand" reward, parents can add the checks over a period of days or weeks. The reward can be claimed only when the proper number of points have accumulated.

The number of checks or points necessary for each reward should be equivalent to the desirability of the treat or activity and should be given according to the difficulty and importance of the assignment tasks. Children can assist in determining what the reward should be, but parents should be largely responsible for deciding its "cost."

Tasks required on the chart should be specific and clearly stated. If the chart does not appear to be helping a child to improve responsibilities, homework, or other behavior, the tasks may be too difficult or the rewards inappropriate. Review both the tasks and the rewards.

Initially, parents might need to gently remind their children of the chart and its contents. Reminders generally become unnecessary after success with the system is achieved.

Parents should be careful about excessive rewards. The rewards should not depart significantly from the chart presented in Chapter 2 showing what children should receive at different ages.

The use of this chart should not prohibit parents from sending a child to an isolated quiet room when misbehavior occurs, if this is a procedure that has worked in the past. Similarly, separation of a child from a brother or sister to prevent fussing or fighting should not be stopped if it has worked in the past.

Through this system, we are talking about a child being able to receive rewards throughout a day even if the last hour of the day is tense, uncomfortable, or unrewarding. This is very good. Too frequently, after a successful day, a child has a devastating last few minutes before bedtime, and the pleasure and achievement of the day is destroyed by the tension or heat of its last moments. This behavior checklist permits parents and children to recall or review positive aspects of the day.

Flexibility can be added to the system, if necessary, for behaviors that are especially difficult for the child to sustain for the entire day, such as not provoking a sibling or staying cheerful. The day can be split into three or four parts, and a point can be given for success in each unit of the day. It is sometimes difficult for a child to sustain a desirable behavior or the absence of an undesirable behavior for a full twelve hours. Therefore, breaking the day into units often becomes necessary. Under these circumstances, parents will be rewarding less than a full day of desirable behavior and permitting the child to see how the behavior "pays off." The hope is that the number of units into which the day has been split can be reduced and a check offered for the entire day.

Double and triple rewards can be given per unit time for behavior that might be particularly important. This will help the child to remember the greater significance attached to certain parental encouragements or admonitions.

Several points are worthy of special note in regard to implementing such a system. It is wise to include one or more behaviors that are already successfully performed by the child. In doing this, the child is "being loaded for success." The entire scheme will seem less difficult, the child will certainly gain reward right from the beginning, and motivation in regard to the system will be higher. Parents and children will also see that there are accomplishments already present that are being recognized and now explicitly rewarded.

A second point concerns the phasing out of this procedure. Recent research indicates that the use of external rewards (such as stars, points, checks, money,) tends to evoke immediate and desired response from children, but that the use of excessive external rewards to gain specific behaviors can undermine a child's internal motivation to perform those behaviors once the rewards are no longer being given. Therefore, phasing out the rewards as soon as possible is wise. The chart-reward system should be viewed as a "primer" for positive behavior.

Phasing out the chart can be done "cold turkey" by simply terminating its use. Generally more successful, however, is an increase in the amount of time or the number of events required to earn a check until the behavior exists and the child is losing interest in the system.

Of course, all children should be periodically rewarded for continued good behavior or cooperation with a warm reminder of how well they are doing and perhaps a treat. Here we are speaking of explicit compliments or rewards that should occur in healthy homes anyway. Theoretically, the successful or cooperative behavior becomes increasingly *self-rewarding* to the child as he or she realizes that it is more fun and less trouble to cooperate with his parents.

Ages Three through Five

The chart for this age group is a sample behavior checklist that can be used with a child in the three to five year range. A chart is often very useful at this age to aid the growth of self-control and self-discipline. These characteristics are increasingly more important as a youngster approaches school age.

Table 2. Sample Behavior Checklist for Three- to Five-Year-Olds

	Mon.	Tues.	Wed.	Thurs.	Fri.	Sat.	Sun.
Toys all approximately in their place "shortly after" dinner							
No provoking of siblings							
Not crossing the street unattended							
Helping mother set the table							
No whining							

Of course, a child of this age cannot read. Parents might cut pictures from magazines to represent the tasks being rewarded so that the child can learn what each line represents and see how he or she is doing. Although five possible examples are given on the chart, children in this age range should generally have no more than three or four tasks on their charts. The tasks should be very specifically and simply described.

Occasionally, the child in the three to five year range will simply accept stars as rewards in and of themselves. This is desirable, but if there are older siblings at home who are also on the behavior list system and require stars or checks as tokens to convert for a treat, the possibility of stars as the final goal for the child in the older age range is slim.

Ages Six through Nine

In this age range, increased self-discipline is necessary. The child is in school and expectations regarding self-control and independent behavior are obviously higher than for younger children. Tasks required on the checklist should be clearly stated and

Table 3.   Sample Behavior Checklist for Six- to Nine-Year-Olds

	Mon.	Tues.	Wed.	Thurs.	Fri.	Sat.	Sun.
Tooth brushing							
Room "straightened" by 7:00 P.M.							
Bike put away in its place by 6:30 P.M.							
Garbage taken out							
Clothes picked up by retirement							
No provoking siblings							
No whining							
Homework completed 6:30 P.M.							

slightly more difficult. No more than six or seven should be asked of a child this age.

Checks or points can be given for the accomplishment of the prescribed behavior, but stars for the nine and often the eight-year-old are frequently seen as childish by the youngster. For children in this age range the accumulation of checks or points can be exchanged for prized activities such as additional television viewing. (For example, one check might be equivalent to ten minutes viewing time.) Or the checks might be worth money. For example, one point could equal four cents and twenty-five points equal a dollar. Parents must be careful that the rewards do not become excessive.

Ages Ten through Twelve

When drawing up a chart for a child in this age range, the parent and the child should come to an agreement about what is

Table 4.   Sample Behavior Checklist for Ten- to Twelve-Year-Olds

	Mon.	Tues.	Wed.	Thurs.	Fri.	Sat.	Sun.
Returning home at reasonably prescribed time							
Completing homework by 7:30 P.M.							
Care for and appropriately store bike							
Successfully avoiding conflict with siblings							
Successfully attending to personal hygiene							
Soiled clothing properly placed in hamper							
Room well cared for by 7:30 P.M.							

required. However, the final decision rests with the parent. Occasionally children in this age range will refuse to cooperate with the system and efforts to encourage them to do so are not successful.

If a child agrees to the chart initially but it does not appear to be helping, the tasks may be too difficult or the rewards may be wrong. It is often helpful and more interesting to change the rewards and responsibilities every few weeks or months.

There should be no more than seven or eight tasks on the chart for a child of this age. Checks, points, or even pennies can be given for the accomplishment of the prescribed behavior, but issuing stars to a youngster in this age range is ordinarily considered demeaning or childish. As with other age groups, the accumulation of checks or points can be converted to either money or prized activities.

Ages Thirteen through Fifteen

The behavior presented in the chart for this age group is representative of the behaviors that the child in the thirteen to fifteen year range should be performing.

Table 5.   Sample Behavior Checklist for Thirteen- to Fifteen-Year-Olds

	Mon.	Tues.	Wed.	Thurs.	Fri.	Sat.	Sun.
Returning home at prescribed times							
Completing homework by 8:00 P.M.							
Successfully mowing the lawn							
Room straightened and clean by 8:00 P.M. each evening							
No conflict with siblings							
Polite interactions with adults							
Proper personal hygiene							

No more than ten items should be on the chart. Money (one to five cents per check) is an acceptable reward, but stars will undoubtedly be seen as childish.

A young teen will often respond to the behavior checklist favorably. In the authors' experience, children of this age often crave the type of structure and clarity of expectations and rewards the checklist offers.

Both parent and child must be responsible for designing the requirements and the rewards at this age. Sometimes children at this age believe that charts are childish. A discussion comparing this "system" to production and efficiency charts in business may be useful. If a child does not enter the system cooperatively, it will probably not be useful; however, parents might be able to gain a commitment that the tasks will be performed without the chart.

6 The Pre-First-Grader

Between three and five years, a child is rapidly changing in terms of interests, developmental skills, aptitudes, attitudes, and relationships with family members. It is an age of rapid transition in which physical growth and improved coordination take place and in which particular attention should be paid by the parent to the child's interests, fears, and activities.

Change during this period is both rapid and erratic. What is true in one week for the three-year-old is not true the next. He or she may show an excessive fear for a particular activity or object and the next day express delight and pleasure with it. This is an entirely normal characteristic for this age, and parents should be careful not to take too seriously a child's statements of desire and intent. At the same time, parents should not allow such children to feel that their desires and attitudes are not important.

As an example, when a three-year-old boy told his parents that he wanted to be a statue when he grew up, the parents thoughtfully praised him for his desire to grow up and "be something," but inside they felt with some dismay that their child had rather dismal vocational aspirations. Of course, within a matter of weeks this same child wanted to be a police officer, and the parents' outward response to this vocational aspiration was the same. If these parents would have attempted to dissuade him from his desire to be a statue through an intellectual discourse, or if they would have ridiculed him for this desire, he would not have understood the explanation and would have been hurt and ashamed.

Play

The development of self-esteem and pride within a child is extremely important at this age. A good deal of the activity that youngsters in this age range expend appears to be free play. But, really, they are choosing to participate in activities in which they feel success and achievement.

There is a considerable amount of modeling that takes place at this age. The youngster is directly attempting to emulate older siblings, parents, or neighbors in terms of interests and activities. A smile, a touch, a word of praise or encouragement can support a child in these modeling activities, and parents should be aware of what they are rewarding in this regard. If the reward is a consequence of modeling undesirable behavior, these undesirable behaviors will likely continue. Similarly, a reward given as a result of desirable modeling behavior will encourage the child to participate in that behavior again.

Caution should be exercised against having children this age involved in activities that are too difficult or unrewarding so that they suffer blows to their self-esteem. That is, children must be protected from significant failures by keeping their recreational activities and ego-builders relatively simple and largely within their areas of strength and competence. Again, it is important to remember that children in this age range change rapidly. One week the child may choose to play with care and the next week may be completely sloppy. A boy may choose to play with dolls and guns one week and help his mother around the house or want to go to work with his daddy the next. Parents should be conscious of the child's current involvement, interests, and participations, and achievement should be praised.

A balance needs to be established between giving youngsters of this age the very limited independence they need on the one hand and providing sufficient structure and control on the other. Children of this age are poor decision-makers. They should not decide their bedtimes or mealtimes and should be given a very limited range of decision-making. The judgment of preschoolers is poor, and they will think nothing of wearing snowsuits on a hot summer day or eating a bag of chocolates instead of a meal for dinner.

Parental Control

Choices given the child should be of the following type: "It is warm outside, which of these two pairs of shorts would you like to wear?" "It is dinner time. Would you like a lot of potatoes or only a few?"

This is the age when a great deal of control can and should be exercised by the thoughtful and concerned parent. The "democratic family" is a very confusing and frustrating social unit in general, but particularly for a youngster in this age range.

The ability to tell right from wrong before the age of five or six is fluid and unpredictable indeed. Parents should not place the three- to five-year-old in a position of having to make judgments of right from wrong. The probability of an incorrect decision is high and the child can face criticism and confusion that can affect development adversely. Parents should be protectors and teachers of children at this age and should not let children get "out on limbs" and set themselves up for failure in this area.

Education

The three- to five-year-old is gathering much information and composing a picture of the world, as immature and incomplete as it may be. Exposure to simple facts through books, games, and other sources is vital. Many children are extremely inquisitive and answers to questions should be given. A word of caution is necessary here, however. Too much information can be given to a child in this age range. If a three-year-old asks where babies come from, a discourse on the physiology of sex and reproduction is not appropriate, even though it might be if the same question were asked by a ten- or eleven-year-old. Typically, a shallow and superficial explanation is all that a three-, four-, or five-year-old can deal with.

Children's inquiries are not only opportunities to provide information but also to give instruction in values: right and wrong ways of doing things. Children should be given information regarding constructive, productive attitudes and values that the parent knows are marks of people we call successful.

A youngster in this age range should be presented with superficial information of either a positive or negative nature. For example, if a child wants to be a police officer as a grown-up and wants to discuss police work with the parent, the child should be presented with its positive aspects: police officers help people, they are working for a living, they wear nice uniforms. Negative aspects can also be presented. For example, being a police officer is dangerous, and police must work at night. To introduce a child of this age to such complex and theoretical issues as the social animosity toward police and the authority they represent will be thoroughly confusing.

It is between three and five that pre-academic types of interests and activities should be emphasized. Children should definitely be read to and permitted to draw. Parental encouragement and a child's achievement in these areas should accelerate by the time a child reaches five years of age, and parent interest and concern for the child's success in a kindergarten should be strong.

It is in kindergarten that social change takes place most rapidly. (But this may begin as early as age three in a nursery school setting.) Cooperation with strangers or relative strangers becomes required and social behavior in a group becomes the norm. The child is taken from the family and placed in a classroom, typically with more structure than the home offers and a narrower range of activities with strong pressures for success. The development of social skills that do not interfere with academic or pre-academic achievement is important.

Parents' Rights

Raising a child requires sensitivity, observation, and constant awareness and concern. But parents have rights, too. Parents should not feel guilty for being human beings and needing time for themselves. If a mother feels ill, she is ill. If a father is tired or preoccupied, he cannot be expected to participate with his child in a way the child may choose and he should not feel guilty for allowing this momentary state of his own humanness to interfere with his function as "a parent." The task of parenting is vitally important but should not be all-consuming. Parents should leave time for recreational activities of their own and that do not involve their children.

Expectations

Expectations are extremely important throughout a person's life, and expectations in this age range are no exception. It should be remembered that children have expectations different from adults. Their understanding of time and place differs from that of adults and a big event for an adult may not be a big event for a child at all. Conversely, what a parent may regard as a negligible situation or event, may be a highlight to a child. Parents should attempt to be aware of their childrens' expectations, their own expectations, and expectations of other people in a child's life, such as grandparents, siblings, and teachers. When there are substantial differences in expectations, discomfort to all involved will result. There will be anxiety, a lack of clarity, and feelings of failure, particularly for the child.

Responsibility should be asked of the child in the three to five year age range. Responsibilities should be extremely simple and nontechnical. Placing clothes in the hamper and keeping toys confined to a particular section of the room are worthwhile responsibilities for most three-year-olds. The four-year-old's responsibilities should be more precise; for example, most toys up off the floor or two sections of the room kept straight, clothes picked up, and the bed straightened.

From approximately the age of five on, some even more precise responsibilities should be provided for the child.

A caution again: If responsibilities are excessive and a demand for accomplishment is made, anxiety, injured self-esteem, and conflict will result. Remember, the preschool youngster's understanding of the world is far different from that of the parents, and a child's expectations and beliefs are typically different from those of an adult.

Bedtime

Bedtime is extremely important in general but particularly so for a child of this age. Many take an afternoon nap. When this occurs, the evening bedtime is often later. If a child does not take a nap, bedtime should be as early as 7:00 P.M. but rarely later than 8:00 P.M. If a child complains that it is still light outside, the complaint can be handled by shifting responsibility for that phenomenon away from the parent: "We are sorry, but that's not our fault. The people who set Daylight Savings Time caused that to happen." Typically, a three- or four-year-old will accept this type of explanation and view the situation as a phenomenon that cannot be controlled.

Bedtime should be a time for some quiet reverie for this age group. It is an opportunity for one or both parents to take the youngster to bed, sit, and chat briefly, perhaps read a story, and in general quiet the child and maintain closeness and warmth.

It has been our experience that on the day a child takes a nap it is somewhat more difficult for him or her to fall asleep in the evening. Many children in this age range reject naps because they want to play. If the parent sees that a child is extremely tired or fussy before or immediately after supper, the child should perhaps be forced to take an afternoon nap.

We have also seen parents who force naps on children who do not need them and then complain about the children not going to sleep at a reasonable hour at night. In these cases, we have recommended eliminating afternoon naps on an experimental basis initially and attempting an earlier bedtime at night. For the four- or five-year-old who still requires a nap but rejects it, the parent can refer to the event as "rest time" and avoid the word "nap." This often works very well.

Bedtimes are important for parents as well as children. The child in the three to five year age range will often wear down a mother during the day and the father who returns from a busy schedule of work can find himself with a frayed wife and become rapidly intolerant himself. When the child's day terminates in the early evening, the parents have valuable time for conversation, entertainment, and separation from the youngster. In the lives of many busy men and women today, unfortunately, it is often the only time available to themselves, and it should be guarded jealously.

Roughhousing

The youngster of this age should receive considerable physical contact from his parents. Wrestling, tussling, tickling, and in general cautious roughhousing is an exceptionally good way for the parent and the child to relate. Physical contact games are easily developed, and most children and parents enjoy them. There are many reasons for tussling with the youngster in this age range including the development of a sense of physical fair play (what is hitting for real and what is hitting for fun) and how far a child can go with a parent physically. It also shows children that they are small and incapable of "defeating" an adult. The parent should permit children to "win" occasionally, however. It is through physical contact that the tenderness, affection, and closeness vital to a loving adult relationship begin.

Young children can be confused over game time and non-game time activities. If parents wrestle with children, get them over-stimulated, and imitate boxing and fighting, they must make it clear when this activity is *really* over. If parents are clear and consistent in communication to their children, the youngsters will be able to discriminate the game and the end of the game. Youngsters should not be encouraged to perform in unsocial ways, such as hitting other children in the face or throwing objects that were meant to stay on a bookcase.

Dressing

Youngsters should begin dressing themselves when they are young, and by age six the average child should be quite accomplished in this activity, with the possible exception of tying shoes. The three-year-old will generally find putting on and taking off pants the easiest of the dressing maneuvers. Taking off socks is relatively easy. Putting on and taking off a shirt, particularly a pullover type, is somewhat more difficult and may not be mastered until age four.

In regard to dressing, we have found the following technique to be most helpful to children. If a child is experiencing difficulty in putting on pants, a proven instructional technique is to dress the child except for pulling up the pants the last three or four inches. Over a series of dressings, the child is obliged to complete more and more of the task. This, in effect, is working backward. The advantage is that the child will always experience success in the completion of the task. The same, of course, is true for pulling on socks, and the child can be initially obliged to draw them up only the last inch and then work backward, leaving two inches to be drawn up, then the heel to be drawn over plus two inches, then the whole foot plus the heel and the two inches, and so on.

Mealtime

We have discovered that mealtime can be particularly important to a family. If the ages of the children permit, mealtime can be an opportunity for the family to review the day or plan for the immediate future. It can be a quiet time and one in which relationships develop and ideas are exchanged. Unless there is a medical reason, children should not be forced to eat excessively if they are naturally light eaters. If they have a narrow range of food desires, they should not be forced to eat undesirables. They may thank their parents later for encouragement to sample a variety of foods, however. Children in the three to five year age range typically do have a narrow range of foods that they choose to eat. Forcing children to eat when they do not care to will often result in unnecessary conflict and unhappiness.

If children at this age become unruly at the dinner table, throwing food or intentionally tipping beverages, and do not respond to a reminder to stop, they could be placed in their rooms for a brief "time-out" until they are ready to rejoin the family. In the home of one of the authors, the child's room is called a "penalty box" for the purpose of removing the child from the family when misbehavior occurs. Even with all of the delightful and exciting toys and activities in the child's room, it becomes the most undesirable area of the house when it is referred to as the "penalty box." It is certainly not overused as a penalty box or the child might find the room progressively more attractive and her father progressively less so.

When children are sent to their rooms because of temper tantrums or other disobedience, parents must remember that a child's understanding and perspective of time is different from that of an adult. Thus a child should not be restricted to a room for more than fifteen minutes, unless the tantrum continues. Sending a child of this age to a room for an hour or more is not advisable. The child may fall asleep, forget the cause of his discipline, become extremely upset for too long a period of time, or enjoy the rewarding aspects of the bedroom.

Caution must be exercised regarding disobedience at the dinner table because the muscle control of such a young child is not good, and accidents will happen. Glasses of milk or juice are often tipped over, and frequently the child is unable to manage eating utensils with a great deal of success. Food occasionally becomes scattered on the table or floor. Parents must be alert to distinguish between the malicious or wanton dumping of foods or beverages, and the accident that occurs as a result of rambunctiousness or horseplay.

There are many simple modifications in a child's meal that will allow the child to feel a part of the family and ensure the success of the meal. Because the three-, four-, and five-year-old does not have the control of his body that an older child or an adult does, beverages and glasses should be only half full, and eating utensils should be smaller. Children should not be given knives with which they could cut themselves. Also, the amount of food children eat does not in any way approach the amount of food adults eat, and much less should be placed on children's plates so that they can finish with a "clean plate" and have a feeling of completion at the end of the meal like the rest of the family.

In any family, discord can occur at the evening meal. Mother has worked hard to prepare a meal, and she is hungry. The children are typically hungry and becoming tired as bedtime is approaching. When father comes home tired, looking forward to an evening of relaxation, and finds tenseness and frayed tempers, the situation may become volatile.

There should be an understanding that dinner time in the home of the young child will sometimes take this tense form. Accommodation and expectation on the parents's part that the people participating in such a fiasco "are not themselves" can be very helpful. If tolerance can be extended and assistance provided, by the time the meal is over, frayed nerves are usually repaired and smiles are again on the family members's faces.

Security Blankets

Many children in the three to five age range show a seemingly excessive attachment to objects such as blankets or favorite dolls. It is often comical to see a five-year-old with a tattered, frayed, dirty, and thoroughly nonfunctional rag that has served as a personal blanket since birth.

These attachments to objects, or "comforters," should not concern the parent of a youngster this age unless they are creating humiliation for the child through criticism from peers or siblings, or interfering with the child's own ability to participate in normal developmental and family functions. In such a case, the most effective way to reduce the reliance on a comforter is to reduce the amount of time the child is allowed to use it so that after two or three weeks the child is no longer allowed to have the comforter outside of his or her own bedroom. If a child this age becomes terrified or insists on keeping the comforter, the issue should not be forced. There should be no problem with the child having a comforter at night; most eventually outgrow the need. Another way to gradually reduce dependency on the comforter is to limit the place that the child can use it to one chair or one area of the house and then work backwards to the bedroom as the only appropriate place for the comforter.

If a comforter such as a blanket is ragged, rather than throw away the entire blanket, gradually allow smaller and smaller pieces to remain with the child. The pieces could be sewed onto a doll or teddy bear that stays in the bedroom. Or occasionally, a child will respond favorably to a parent offering to give the blanket to "poor people who have no blanket at all." If the child is pleased by this idea, the blanket can be removed. The child will feel extremely generous in relinquishing this vital object to someone in need.

Tantrums

Tantrums are common, but not universal, for this age group. The children are exerting themselves and are finding the world a frustrating and at times disappointing place. They do not have the verbal facility or the communication skills to express disappointment or frustration, and the common alternative is the temper tantrum. Tantrums in this age range normally can be handled by physically taking children to a "time-out room" and requiring them to stay there until two to five minutes *after* the tantrum stops. Parents must be careful not to reward a child by becoming upset or lecturing while the child is being taken to the room, and parents must not stand near the room to see if the child comes out, thus rewarding the tantrum behavior. Parents must go to another part of the house and let the child scream as long as necessary.

The authors have suggested to parents that they turn on the phonograph or sing loudly to themselves to try to block out the pain which they themselves feel in sympathy for the child. A child will occasionally become extremely angry and wreck his room.

When a daughter of one of the authors was three years old, she was placed in her room for a tantrum. She threw toys and even removed the mattress from her bed. This behavior did not dissuade her parents from making use of the "time-out room" in the future, however.

Children who behave in a way that may be physically harmful to them may have to be held during a tantrum. Caution should be exercised that this is not a reward to the child and that it does not promote more temper tantrums. The parent must be sure that there are many more positive situations in which the child is held; that is, when tantrums are not taking place.

Whining and Fussing

Another problem common in the three to five year age range is whining and feeling out of sorts.

If the whining is taking place in the late afternoon, the child might be hungry. This is especially likely if it has been a long time since he or she has eaten. A small snack will probably correct this situation. Also, the bedtime schedule should be reviewed to determine whether the child is getting enough sleep.

If whining is persistent and excessive—five, six, or more times a day over several weeks—the parent should contact a pediatrician to see if there are physical problems. If whining and feeling out of sorts takes place at certain times of the year, allergies may be the cause.

When a child with a tendency to whine speaks in an even voice without complaining, parents should reward that behavior by smiling, praising, and following through on the request if it is at all reasonable. A request associated with whining should be ignored. The child should soon understand that whining does not achieve what he or she desires. See Chapter 4 for ways to reduce the frequency, intensity, and duration of whining.

Sibling Rivalry

Sibling rivalry is common, and between three and five a child often becomes enmeshed in conflicts with siblings. A child of this age may be somewhat of a pest by getting into an older brother's or sister's possessions, rooms, and activities. Parents must be careful that the child at this age is not manipulating an older child and pretending to be hurt. If there are older siblings, the younger child may be spoiled by them, as well as by the parents, and want to stay in the limelight. Sibling rivalry, even continuing for hours at a time, is natural and usually will dissipate if the parents can stay out of the situation.

Many times conflict occurs to bring the parent into the middle of a disagreement so that one or more of the children involved can obtain parental attention. One of the best ways for parents to avoid participation is for them to separate the children. This often serves as a punishment because while they appear to be at great odds to the parents, they are usually enjoying this "game" and will work more cooperatively for the pleasure of playing together and being together. As a rule of thumb, unless a child is being ridiculed, hit, or property is being destroyed, parents should generally avoid involvement in sibling conflict.

Children should be allowed to argue, disagree, and settle disputes among themselves, but it is important to set a rule that hitting—especially on the face and head—will be punished. If these types of disagreements and arguments are continuous, taking place on an average of more than five times per day, then parents should look at each child who is engaged in this type of negative interaction and go through the checklist of developmental keys and disciplinary mistakes outlined in Chapter 3 to determine the conditions that may be affecting the child's self-concept. Insufficient individual time with each parent and the introduction of increased privileges and responsibilities are often causes here.

Much sibling rivalry occurs when one child is attempting to accomplish a task in a public or community area of the house. The child should be encouraged to remove this activity (puzzle, pickup sticks, coloring book, for example) and play in another area of the house where he or she is not underfoot or is "fair game" for siblings. Children should have their own private area of the home where other children are not permitted without permission. It is in that area that the child can play uninterrupted, and it should be made clear to all siblings that this is a private area. A most convenient location is the child's room or a section of it.

A three- to five-year-old child who is restless and has been corralled in a car for a long period can provoke many types of sibling and parental conflicts. Promptly stopping the car and making it entirely clear that such disruptive behavior will not be tolerated is the best procedure.

Sibling rivalry and other conflicts are common in the early morning or immediately before dinner or bedtime. Children, particularly in the three to five year age range, tire easily and when they are tired or hungry their tolerance for frustration is greatly reduced. Under these conditions, the probability of conflict is much higher. The parent would be wise to be alert for such situations and try to keep schedules and demands relatively low until these physical states can be modified. Many a virtual "life-and-death" conflict immediately before supper is totally forgotten as soon as the meal is completed. Unless physical damage, ridicule, or property damage is occurring, parents should remember that within a brief period the three- to five-year-old will usually forget the conflict and the parents should also.

Sibling rivalry in a child who is three to five years old can occur with an older brother or sister. A three-year-old is mobile and is interested in the activities of an older sibling. A younger child will emulate the interests and activities of an older child. Such young children cannot be expected to deal as effectively with situations as an eight-year-old sibling, yet they may try to perform as well. They need to be protected by the parent not from their attempts to emulate but from the failures they will encounter.

The situation can be compounded if an older child feels resentment about a younger child's participation and if the older child feels pre-empted. Frustration results in both the older child, who feels that the younger child should not be so participating, and the younger child, who feels unable to perform with the proficiency of the older child. We believe it is important to encourage independent areas of activities and successes for each child in the family. This becomes particularly important if there is a young child who cannot be successful in activities already mastered by an older child.

Sibling rivalry occurs because of children's attempts to be identical with one another in a family or from parents placing more reward and pride in one child's activities than in those of another. Parents should be cautious and very observant in this area.

Toilet-Training and Bed-Wetting

Children are usually toilet-trained between ages two and three. It is not unusual for a child not to be toilet trained by the age of three, however, particularly a male. Some children become fearful of "potty" training, and it is necessary to educate the child to overcome this fear. In toilet-training itself, it is often desirable to have the child complete defecation on the toilet or defecate immediately so that sitting on the toilet becomes connected with the defecation. It is also helpful, especially if problems develop, to chart the times when defecation and urination take place so that the parents could know appropriate times to have the child use the toilet. A child will often enjoy placing a star on a blank piece of paper every time he uses the toilet properly. This paper can be placed on a wall next to or near the toilet.

Probably toilet noises, unpleasant odors, and the fact that the child sees "part of himself" voided and disposed of occasionally give rise to fears of the bathroom. If the child becomes afraid of the bathroom, several procedures can be used. The bathroom will evoke less anxiety in a child if he or she performs other more enjoyable activities there—using favored games and toys on the floor, for example. Comforting objects such as favorite books can also be introduced. If the child will not enter the bathroom even to participate in attractive activities, a potty can be used in other more comfortable locations in the house until the child becomes comfortable in the bathroom. (See Chapter 4 for a more detailed discussion of childhood fears.)

Bed-wetting during ages three to five should not be considered a problem. If a child is wetting the bed at this age, much encouragement for a dry night should be given, but punishment by the parents should be avoided for "an accident." If bed-wetting is a problem, tactics such as avoiding liquid intake after 6:00 P.M. and making certain that the child has gone to the bathroom before retiring should be implemented.

Sociability

In regard to the issue of sociability in this age range, there are general trends that will in all likelihood persist for some time. There is a general rule of thumb concerning the age position a child holds in the family. Older children tend to be more shy, socially hesitant, reluctant, and conservative than younger children, who are more aggressive, outspoken, socially pushy, and gregarious. These differences frequently cut across sex lines, although girls are somewhat more passive than boys in terms of their social aggressiveness.

Unless aggressiveness or shyness is excessive, parents should generally be able to predict a child's behavior in a given situation. Anticipating a certain response will prevent disappointment. Invariably, as a child grows older and experiences more successes and achievements, parents will find the shy child taking more risks and the aggressive child showing more restraint.

If a young child's social group is chosen with caution (proper school, proper neighborhood, proper restriction from undesirable children, for example), the group will tend to place pressure on the youngster and educate him or her about getting along with other children. Children in this age range, however, should rarely be left unattended in groups with other children because their level of social understanding is slim.

Occasionally a child in this age range will display certain types of social adjustment difficulties. There may be excessive shyness or fear of playing with children, or an aggressiveness that prevents the child from being accepted. Proper school behavior must be rewarding to children. They must see that they will be rewarded when they do not deprive others, hurt others, and when they choose to participate. If a child is fearful, it may be that the child's companions are older or that they are more mature and aggressive even if they are the same age. Perhaps a companion is beating or ridiculing the child.

If the problems are taking place only at school, it may be that the child is experiencing a developmental deficiency and feels uncomfortable in school. Such difficulties are often seen in the "immature child" who is not ready for many of the activities of nursery school or kindergarten. They occur more frequently in boys and girls with birthdays late in the year and who are thus actually six to nine months younger than their classmates. The child who is immature may need to be held back one grade. And unpleasant as this may seem, it is better done early in the child's school career than late.

Sometimes a child is more aggressive at play or more fearful at home than at school. But this can result from a fear in school. Fear of a teacher or fear that he or she is not keeping up with the work will sometimes cause a child to restrain feelings and emotions at school. They then may be released vigorously and aggressively at home because the child feels more comfortable there. Typically, there are enough situations in which a child's social conduct can be observed by parents for them to decide which situations cause the child to behave in fearful or aggressive ways.

Is the child happier and less aggressive in the summer and on weekends? If so, perhaps the school itself is producing the irritability or fear. What about other situations in the community? Does the child behave well in playground activities or at religious services and school? In these other situations there is usually less academic stress with a substantial amount of social interaction.

It is commonly believed that if a child is aggressive in school he or she must be aggressive at home and vice versa. This is not true.

As a consequence of this fallacy, teachers and parents sometimes suspect each other of covering up for or being overly critical of the child.

The development of self-esteem and self-confidence is extremely important in this age range. Three- to five-year-old children should be expected to be afraid at times. If they are comforted and encouraged, and the situation is dealt with lightly, the normal fears of water, the dark, animals, bad dreams, and losing their parents will be rapidly overcome. Parents should be careful that the normal fears of three- to five-year-olds are not rewarded by *excessive* parental support. When this occurs, the parents are, in fact, *teaching* the child to be afraid by rewarding the fear.

Learning Problems

Although specific learning disabilities are rarely noticed before children enter school, the problem does exist before then. Technology is permitting us to identify a learning disability in a child who is not old enough for school. However, in the absence of valid test information or the professional who can evaluate the presence of such a problem, extreme caution must be exercised.

A learning disability, as we operationally define it, is a lag in the development of certain types of learning abilities in certain specific areas. Because the three- to five-year-old is developing at an extremely accelerated rate, certain areas of development may lag behind others at any particular time. For example, we have observed children reducing their interest and competence in gross motor areas while accelerating speech development. This is a fully normal phenomenon in the development of the young child.

Parents may, however, look for two signs that suggest the presence of a learning disability and then seek sound professional assistance to determine if a disability is present. First, hyperactivity that causes the child to spend very little time concentrating on specific tasks or activities may indicate a learning disability. We frequently characterize this activity level in terms of a "hyper-reactivity," which implies that occasionally the child can sit for extended periods of time but under stimulation, hyperactivity occurs. Second, a noticeable lag in the development of skills such as talking, crawling, playing ball, coloring, or a lack of interest in being read to from books in general. Any one of these signs may be significant. If parents have questions, they should seek competent professional advice.

Preschools

Two generations ago, the youngster who was three to five years old typically did not attend school. A generation ago, kindergarten classes became more popular and the five-year-old began to attend school. Today, many three-year-olds are beginning school activities at an earlier age by attending nursery schools. Parents seeking a nursery school should do so carefully.

We have found that many pediatricians and psychologists have knowledge concerning reputable nursery schools, and their advice should be sought. There are good nursery schools and poor nursery schools. The good schools generally provide a considerable amount of stimulation and offer opportunities for children to participate in groups and associate with each other to a great extent. Nursery schools for four-year-olds that have the strongest curriculum generally introduce children to coloring with crayons, the basic use of pencils, and books through both teacher reading to the children and the children being permitted to look through books freely.

It is important, however, that three- and four-year-olds spend most of their school day in "free play" activities. Such children should not be placed in a "school" for more than fifteen hours a week unless it is *absolutely* necessary.

It's also best not to place a child into a nursery school or day-care center before age three. The love, attention, and affection that a parent provides is rarely replaced by a nursery school for children younger than three, regardless of the amount or source of funding for a preschool program or the way in which it is advertised. It is occasionally absolutely necessary for a mother with a very young child to become employed. Nursery school placement for a child younger than three should be made with much investigation and competent professional assistance.

In strong kindergarten programs for four- and five-year-olds, academic readiness begins to play a more important role. Toward the end of the strong kindergarten program, children are introduced to the type of structure that they will experience in the first grade. More orderliness is called for, and academic skills may be taught. Frequently, the child in kindergarten is taught the alphabet and numbers, for example, and occasionally the five-year-old learns to write portions of the alphabet (usually in a primitive form) and to count.

A strong kindergarten should be able to communicate with parents concerning a youngster's readiness to enter the first grade and make sound projections regarding the child's ability to handle the first-grade curriculum.

Children who are four or five are in a "get ready to read stage." Three- and four-year-olds enjoy looking at picture books by themselves and having stories read to them. At five, they attempt to identify letters, words, and phrases that are frequently repeated such as sounds of the animals, or familiar signs such as Stop and Go. Some five-year-olds may read letters in sequence and ask what they spell, or they may associate a single letter with the beginning of a familiar name.

If a child shows no interest in books or is inattentive when being read to, perhaps the following readiness activities would be helpful.

Present the child with a box of colored beads to be sorted by color. When this has been accomplished, the child may sort them by shapes or sizes. Colored blocks may also be used to sort by color. After the child is able to successfully sort the beads and blocks in various ways, he or she should be shown a bead pattern, which the parent forms on a string. The exposure time should be about two or three seconds per bead in the pattern. After viewing the pattern for a designated length of time, the child should reproduce the pattern on his shoestring. The procedure for colored block designs should be the same as the bead patterns.

Children should have many experiences with puzzles. They should start with inset-type puzzles of only one object and progress to several objects. The next puzzles should be those that show the outline of the pieces on the board after individual pieces have been removed. This offers some help to a child who may be having visual perception problems. From this type of puzzle, the child may be exposed to regular puzzles; however, regular puzzles should be of fewer pieces and the number increased gradually.

By four or five years of age, children should have learned to walk down steps in the normal manner. However, if they must place both feet on each step, they should be given some help in the form of "large motor training."

For this training, parents should start with "Angels in the Snow." The child lies on his back on the floor with his arms at his sides and legs together. On the count of *one,* he spreads his legs twelve inches and moves his arms perpendicular to his body. On the count of *two,* his legs spread widely, and his arms meet above his head. The count of *three* brings him to the same position as the count of one, and the count of *four* completes the cycle with a return to the starting position. It may be necessary for some children to start by only moving one leg while the parent holds the other. The arm movements should be added after the leg movements can be performed rhythmically.

When the child can do "Angels in the Snow" with the limbs at an equal distance from the body and in smooth rhythm, he or she is ready for "Jumping Jacks." "Jumping Jacks" are the same as "Angels in the Snow," but they are performed in a standing position. Hopping—on one foot at a time and with both feet—can also be practiced by the child.

The next activity in the large motor sequence is the "Walking Board Exercise." In preparation for this exercise, children should learn to walk a line on the floor making sure to place heel to toe and keeping their eyes focused on a target straight ahead. The "Walking Board" is simply two smooth, six-foot, two-by-four-inch boards placed end-to-end flat on their four inch sides. The child should practice going forward, backward, sideways, and forward to middle and turning around. These activities should be practiced slowly. Walking the board rapidly does not indicate good balance.

Ready to Write

Some children show an interest in learning to print their names at four or five years of age. They should learn to use both upper and lower case letters from the first attempt and should write with a jumbo crayon on large paper.

If the child has difficulty holding or writing with the jumbo crayon, he or she may not have developed sufficient fine motor coordination. In this event, writing should be discouraged and the following activities should be done to improve the child's coordination. To develop motor skills and finger dexterity, have the child practice snapping clothespins on and off a piece of rope. The palm should be downward during this process using fingers and thumb in a pincer movement. As muscle control develops, the child should use only one finger at a time with the thumb.

Other activities that will strengthen the muscles necessary for writing are mixing and working with clay or similar substance, finger-painting, folding napkins for the table, using scissors, and unscrewing and replacing tops of various-sized jars and bottles.

Thus far we have presented exercises to strengthen weak muscles. Another problem some children encounter in writing is poor eye-to-hand coordination. Games such as "Ring Toss," "Horseshoes," or "Bean Bag Toss" are helpful for improving far-point eye-to-hand coordination. A child should start close enough to the target to ensure success, probably one or two feet, and gradually move back as skill increases.

For near-point coordination, have the child connect dot pictures, trace plain objects, cut staying on the lines, and use lacing boards or sew large cross-stitches on unbleached muslin.

If a child has developed sufficiently and shows interest in writing, an alphabet chart will help parents teach the child the correct directions for forming letters. Thus, the child will not have to "unlearn" poor writing habits in first grade. (See Figure 3.)

Before entering first grade, most children learn to count by rote without difficulty. If a child has difficulty learning to count by rote past a certain number, however, or if he or she consistently skips a particular number, then the child's body movement should be

Figure 3. Alphabet Chart

involved in the learning process. Have the child count while hopping or jumping, skipping or walking on numbered stepping stones, walking a "number" line, or watching moving objects such as large beads or blocks.

Number usage is an abstract skill, and the child should learn to correlate the visual number with its name as early as possible. A number may be shown and said to a child simultaneously. Ask the child to stand on a stepping-stone of that number, or show and say the number and ask the child to choose the number that looks identical from a small group of numbers, perhaps three or four initially. After learning to correlate the visual images and the names of several numbers, the child can start taking the numbers and placing them in sequence as he counts by rote.

Of all the skills a child has acquired before entering first grade, perhaps some of the most important are auditory. If a child has difficulty discriminating between sounds or following verbal commands, first grade can be frustrating. To help prepare the five-year-old in this area, have the child turn away while familiar sounds are produced, such as clapping, stomping, crumpling paper, or the sounds of an animal. If the child identifies each sound correctly, the parent might say pairs of words and ask the child if the same word or two different words were said each time.

In addition, parents should give simple verbal commands, starting with one request and progressing to two and three requests in each command. For example: (1) turn around; (2) hop on one foot, then sit down; (3) stand up, then walk to the door, then hop two times.

Parents should repeat nursery rhymes over and over until the child can supply deleted sequences or can repeat the rhymes from memory with occasional prompting.

A final suggestion is for parents to help a child learn and repeat "finger plays." Books of finger plays may be found at public libraries (e.g., *Finger and Action Rhymes* by Mevelle B. McGuide).

Even though samples of printing are included in this chapter, it should not be assumed that children must learn to write at this age. Five-year-olds should not be forced into a formal learning situation either at home or in kindergarten. Kindergarten should be a time of social development and building of concepts, not a time for getting down to the nitty-gritty of learning.

Allowance

Do not anticipate that a child in the three to five year age range will understand the value of money or the significance or purchasing items with money. Even so, it is important for the child to begin learning that money has value. A nickel a week (with a parental subsidy) can purchase an interesting goody or small toy, however, and the child will feel as if he or she is spending personal money for its purchase. Allowance at this age should be simply given, at a prescribed time. If the child is misbehaving or uncooperative at that moment delay the allowance until he or she is calm so that misbehavior is not inadvertently rewarded. The acquisition of this five cents should not be made contingent on his cooperativeness or any other specific behavior. This is obviously different than for the older child where more demand should be placed upon him for responsible and consistent behavior.

One to One

Remember, one-to-one time between a parent and a child is necessary for proper development. It represents an excellent way to prevent and solve family problems.

Ideally, the father and mother should spend at least two twenty-minute periods per week with each child in total or near isolation from other siblings. They should do something that the child enjoys (and, preferably, that the parent also enjoys) and that is not goal-oriented or perfectionistic or competitive. The parent should assume a guiding but absolutely nonjudgmental and uncritical role.

A child may build a model car and put the wheels on the roof. This is excellent because it gives the parent an opportunity to demonstrate that the *only* goal of their time together is to have fun and enjoy each other. This time is in addition to any other time spent with the child which does not meet the ideal criteria above.

7 The Early School Years

The child aged six through nine is in a critical stage of development. It is at this age that children first enter competitive situations that approximate those that will face them for the rest of their lives. Grades in school, competency on athletic fields, appearance, and social skills take on considerable significance. The child leaves the protected environment of the home for the first time and deals with children from homes with differing values and backgrounds.

In this age range, parents should seek a school for a child that will provide the youngster with peers relatively similar in upbringing, values, morals, and integrity.

There will be ample opportunity to learn about other values and morals as the youngster grows older. A child between the ages of six and nine is not in a position to accurately judge right from wrong.

Values and Morals

Certainly, exposure to other aspects of life, cultures, and morals is important to an individual's development. But if exposure takes place in this age range, when there is insufficient understanding of the "parents' way," it will be confusing at best and destructive to the integrity of the family at worst.

It is worthwhile at this point to mention that values—by which we mean the ability to judge right from wrong—are first understood with clarity by the six-to-nine-year-old.

Values unite young and old and we believe that values are at the core of the family unit. Values often underlie unity, purpose, religion, nationality, and certainly the family. Many sad and regretful parents of children who are sixteen, seventeen, and eighteen years old, whose values are strikingly different from those of the parents, can trace the moral and attitude separation to the age range between six and nine, when the child was thrust into a social peer group that maintained values and morals different from those of the family.

Peer Groups

It is in this age range that children begin to broaden their peer groups by necessity and affiliate more directly with children from other homes. The children with whom the child is associating at school will rarely be known by the parents. It is acceptable for a parent to insist on knowing more about other children in the classroom. Such devices or events as birthday parties, Halloween parties, and Christmas parties are effective ways to get to know a child's classmates and their parents.

Social Problems

Social problems that occur in this age range typically take the form of excessive shyness or aggressiveness. Either problem should be addressed by consulting with teachers about the form that the problem takes and the techniques teachers have used to try to correct the inappropriate behavior.

If the problem is simple and there are no obvious environmental or circumstantial factors causing it, a direct behavioral approach using rewards for the absence of the undesirable behavior can be attempted.

If the excessive behavior continues, professional assistance, initially through a pediatrician, should be sought. A referral may be made to a professional psychologist.

The shy or withdrawn child can typically be lost in the classroom. Because he or she is showing no disruptive problem and commanding no attention, the child's confusion may go unnoticed by the teacher. The aggressive child will be identified as a troublemaker in school, the "squeaky wheel" who commands attention and assistance. But if parents suspect that their child might be excessively shy, it may be necessary for them to initiate the school contact.

Public vs. Private Education

Based on our observations and numerous national reports in recent years, it seems evident that public schools have experienced progressively more complicated problems and that the quality of public education has deteriorated. The reasons for the decreased quality of public schools are many. (See Chapter 2.) Because they have slipped, public schools have become more concerned with communication between child and parents and with discipline and control. Because of financial difficulties, they have arrived at "innovative new techniques," which include trying to teach children in "open" classrooms, multipurpose classrooms, and multi-school schools.

In some areas of the United States, figures show that approximately one child in six at the elementary school level attends a private school. This is a significant increase in the past several years but does not tell the full story. Many of the parents who have removed their children from public education to private education did so after observing the declining status of public schools: the decreased effectiveness of teaching, the decreased amounts of money spent directly on teaching, the decreased discipline in the classrooms, the absence of neighborhood schools over which parents can have control and in which they can be directly involved.

A simple review of the names of parents whose children attend private schools reveals that many are community leaders whose previous involvement with public schools was significant and whose children were certainly school contributors. Many of these parents have spoken out for integration and excellence in public education but have chosen private schools for their children, believing they have a great deal more to offer today. There is little doubt that this is a major blow to public education—both because of the loss of these students and because of the loss of these parents.

Much effort and concern must be expended to improve the quality of public education. At the present time, however, it appears that in some areas of the country, a well-chosen private school offers the most relevant and sound education for children.

Study Habits

The development of proper study habits and positive attitudes toward schoolwork is very important at this early age. Frequently, schools do not teach appropriate study habits and this responsibility falls to the parents. Children should be provided with an acceptable, quiet place of their own to perform schoolwork, and homework should be performed within a specific time period. It should be rare for the first-grader to spend more than twenty minutes on a single day's homework assignment, the second-grader should spend no more than thirty minutes, and the third-grader should spend no more than forty minutes on an average.

Homework should not be left until immediately before bedtime, as it is frequently used as a manipulative device by children. An acceptable time for homework is immediately after school, perhaps after a half-hour break. If a child has a strong urge to play after school, he or she should be called in approximately forty-five minutes before dinner to complete the homework assignment. This scheduling will develop a positive attitude toward conservation of time and consolidation of efforts, which is obviously essential in successful adult life.

A child should be sitting up (more or less straight) while doing homework. The television set should be turned off or out of hearing in another room. Siblings should not interfere or play with the child doing homework. Particularly for the younger child, parents should review the completed assignment to make certain that it has been done properly. This becomes especially important with a child who is showing a resistance to academic work or who has displayed a learning disability. Teachers will give directions too rapidly or with insufficient example so that a child does not understand what is required.

If a child is in a school that does not require homework, a special arrangement may be worked out whereby he or she can do some homework either by the parents's assignment or the school making an exception for the child to do homework. If the child believes that he or she is being discriminated against, it should be explained that the homework in this instance is a parent or family decision that has nothing to do with the child's performance or ability in school. We believe that homework is important because it teaches appropriate study habits, the importance of school, and responsibility toward academic performance. It also lends itself to a communication bridge between school and home that enables parents to better understand what is happening at school.

Lags in Development

An astute first-grade teacher will notice a child who lags behind in the development of skills necessary for academic achievement, such as fine motor and large motor skills.

To prevent a crisis, assistance from a trusted pediatrician, friends, neighbors, or a clergyman should be sought to determine if the problem is sufficient to warrant professional attention.

The development of physical and mental skills necessary for successful academic performance is extremely individualized, and frequently a youngster is "age ready" but not "skill ready." That is, he or she cannot perform the physical and mental activities (not necessarily academic) that most children of the age group can. The absence of such basic skills—not absence of intelligence—may prevent a child from succeeding in school.

Early intervention can prevent great pain for the family, the parents, and the child. The story of Johnny, which is found in Chapter 2, is not intended to alarm parents. But it does present a clear possibility of what can happen, and what has happened, because of a developmental lag that has gone untreated.

It is during this age that the overwhelming majority of children with learning disabilities come to the attention of the professional counselor. Unfortunately, many of the school systems that are offering ungraded classrooms, or are simply passing children along and permitting them to "work at their own levels," are not identifying youngsters with learning disabilities. There is much assistance to offer a child who shows a developmental learning lag in this age range, and we have found that the earlier the intervention takes place the better. A list of problems shown by a child with a learning disability can be found in Chapter 2.

Competent professional assistance should be sought for the child with learning problems and referral should be made initially through the family pediatrician, clergyman, or trusted friends. There are specialists who work with the learning-disabled child. Many school systems have added "learning disability specialists." In our experience caution should be exercised regarding the quality and ability of their performance and credentials.

Often these specialists are restricted by school policy from dealing with any but the most obvious and severe forms of learning problems. Because these specialists are rarely qualified to evaluate intellectual and personality factors, their "diagnosis" and "treatment" may be limited.

Parents should not hesitate to question the education and background, as well as credentials and certification, of such a specialist. If parents would prefer not to risk being labeled "troublemakers" by asking such incendiary questions, a trusted pediatrician or clergyman can make the inquiry.

Although most children with learning disabilities are identified in this age range, we frequently find that learning disabilities in girls are detected later. The reason for this appears to be that girls are often more passive, charming, and cause fewer difficulties in the classroom. Often the difficulty is not recognized until a girl enters junior high school. It is at this point—when reading, spelling, and writing become necessary prerequisites for academic performance, and not subjects that are taught—that the child begins to fail significantly. Of course, the girl in the six to nine year age range should be closely observed by her parents and if academic skills are not forthcoming at her level of ability, professional assistance should be sought.

Sibling Rivalry

Sibling rivalry at this age is more sophisticated than that of younger children. Often it occurs because of territorial encroachment, and parents should protect a child's personal territory.

Frequently, youngsters feel slighted if no particular area of success belongs to them, and they may strike out in a resentful, frustrated fashion at siblings they believe to be receiving more attention, affection, or success.

The child at this age is still young enough to be a bothersome pest to older brothers and sisters and may not have sufficient patience with younger siblings. (The same procedures regarding sibling rivalry outlined in Chapter 6 will generally hold true at this age level. However, children of this age have additional sources of frustration because they have a broader level of interaction outside the home with peers and at school.)

It is important for the parent not to be manipulated into judging who started a particular disagreement or which child violated a rule when the parent has not seen this personally. A child should not be permitted to "tattle" on another child, and tattling should be ignored as much as possible.

If the origin of a disagreement is not observed by the parent, no judgment should be made concerning its origin. It can be pointed out to the children that they are not being punished because they had a disagreement, but rather because screaming, yelling, hitting, or whatever took place is against the rules and that both children or all children who were involved in the screaming, yelling, or hitting are responsible. A child who professes he or she is absolutely not responsible can be reminded that there are better ways to handle conflicts.

If three children are involved in constant harassment of each other, then group pressure can be introduced. Positive and negative consequences can be distributed when all three children go for a morning (perhaps only part of a morning), afternoon, or evening without screaming or fighting. Greater rewards can be given for a full day of good behavior. A check might be made on a chart when the children have had a good morning, afternoon, or evening, and when ten checks are received, a special trip or other reward can be introduced. These checks are always on a cumulative basis. The chart is never used so that a number of checks are required in a row with the result that the children could lose all of their checks when they reached nine because they had a bad morning immediately before they reached the tenth check.

Automobile trips frequently present difficult sibling rivalry problems and on a trip of some length children at this age may have to be spanked if they do not respond to the threat of punishment when the family stops in the evening. Punishment may be the withholding of privileges such as television-viewing time (for example, one half hour per violation), or swimming time.

Physical Contact

The child in this age range is still in need of physical contact from parents and the same issues discussed in the three to five year range pertain here regarding physical contact. Physical closeness, gentleness, and tenderness should be sought by both parents from the child. Wrestling, tussling, and tickling with both parents is important. Of course, additional caution needs to be exercised by the parent engaging in wrestling or tussling with a youngster in the six to nine age range because of the child's level of sophistication and growing strength. The "attack" of the three-year-old carries fewer dangers for the parent than that of the nine-year-old.

The eight- or nine-year-old may be suspicious of "babyish" games, and children usually begin to give up sitting on their parents' laps during this age. They may occasionally choose to sit on a parent's lap but will frequently reject the opportunity, occasionally with vehemence. Certainly, there are many opportunities for the parent to put an arm around the child while watching television, walking, or at other relaxed times.

Habits

At this age, comforters such as blankets or dolls or teddy bears become progressively more obtrusive, and opportunity for ridicule from siblings and peers increases. Frequently at this age, the child is being asked to spend nights at the homes of friends, and we have known a number of children who restrict themselves from this activity because of embarrassment about their comforters.

If a comforter continues to be used in this age range, a stronger look must be taken at the many school, neighborhood, family, and self-esteem factors of the child. If these are being satisfied, then the need for the security blanket should drop out, with only the habit remaining as a cause for the use of the comforter. This should be eliminated rather rapidly through the technique of reducing the amount of usage or place of usage and also positive reward for reduced usage.

Nail-biting, thumb-sucking, and nose-picking are frequently problems. The child should be advised that these are not bad things, but that they should be done in the privacy of the child's room and not in public. They can be reduced by positive consequences as the parent checks the child on a random basis and uses a chart to record behavior. Negative practice can be used for five minutes, three times per day, in front of a mirror. The child completes the full cycle of thumb-sucking, for example, to become aware of it. The child should place the thumb in his or her mouth and then place the hand completely down to the side, doing this as many times as possible during a five minute interval. This is not a punishment, but a technique that has proven effective in terminating these undesirable behaviors. It is not meant to humiliate the child and should be done with only the child and a parent present.

Dressing

It is between the ages of six and nine that a child begins to take personal responsibility for getting dressed. For six- and perhaps seven-year-olds, the parents should present a limited choice of clothing to the youngster. An entire closet of clothing should not be presented. The child should be given a choice of two or three different appropriate outfits.

Occasionally, a child will dawdle or complain of not knowing what to wear in the morning. This can frequently be averted by laying out clothing the night before and explaining that this is what the child is to wear in the morning.

By the time a youngster is eight or nine, considerable latitude in terms of clothing choices should be given; however, caution must be exercised that the child is not choosing inappropriate clothing for school, religious activities, or important occasions.

Typically, with the eight- or nine-year-old, all buttoning, zipping, and tying skills are present. Children should wear clothing similar to the clothes of their parents. That is, attractive outfits should be worn to important occasions and school, and these should be "dress-up" times.

We firmly believe that the youngster in this age range who attends school dressed in a sloppy fashion—even though the school might permit this to occur—is not dressing in a fashion that encourages self-discipline or with an eye toward what one should wear to work in an adult world. A person in business, for example, dresses differently for work than for play.

Hygiene

Preschoolers generally do not have proper independent hygiene skills because their motor control is poor and their understanding of the necessity for good personal hygiene is insufficient. By the time a child reaches the age of six, however, personal hygiene skills should be handled competently with parental monitoring of brushing the teeth, combing hair, and washing the body—especially the ears!

Modesty

Children at this age will periodically become more modest of their bodies, sometimes to an excessive degree. An eight-year-old will occasionally refuse to dress or undress in front of siblings or parents, even of the same sex. One of the authors is reminded of the time when his eight-year-old daughter spent an entire vacation dressing and undressing in motel closets, feeling terribly threatened by her three-year-old brother's attempts to open the closet door.

Mealtimes

The child in the six to nine age range is able to assume a considerable amount of responsibility for assisting at mealtime. The child's help should be sought periodically to set the table, help Mother put out the food, and clear the table. Mealtime should be a quiet time, and distractions such as the television set and neighborhood friends should be avoided. Children should be obliged to remain seated for the entire meal unless excused, and expected to sit up straight, eat with utensils, and with proper table manners.

Running Away

Sometimes children at this age threaten to run away when they meet irreconcilable or non-negotiable resistance from the family. The significance of "running away from home" for a child of this age is entirely different than for a sixteen- to eighteen-year-old making the same threat. When the threat is made or the action is about to be taken, the time can frequently be used by the parent to discuss feelings, family standards, and negotiable as well as non-negotiable rules to which the family adheres.

Occasionally, parents can help the child pack, thereby "calling the bluff," and even permit the child to leave for a period of time without checking on his or her whereabouts. However, caution should be the watchword here, and the child should not be permitted to wander too far from home. When the child returns, parents can make it clear that even though they did not want the child to leave home, they did want him to experience what it was like. In our experience, most children do not wander far but seat themselves on their suitcases outside the house, behind a tree, or behind a neighbor's house.

Parents should not panic during these times and become either too solicitous or too serious. Frequently, a child in this situation is really asking whether the parents care, and the opportunity should be given when the child returns to discuss why he or she is upset. The child is experiencing a crisis and should be treated with respect. Parents, however, must not allow themselves to be manipulated. They should realize that their child is not, in fact, going to run away from home and that the situation is not as serious as the child wants them to believe.

Bedtime Television-Viewing

Bedtimes for children in this age range should be rigidly fixed but flexibly maintained. In our experience, the six-, seven-, and often the eight- and nine-year-old require as much sleep at night as younger children, particularly during the school week. As with other age groups, we believe that bedtimes are important as anchors for children and often essential for parents, who require time for themselves after the children are in bed.

Another important reason for maintaining reasonable bedtimes for children in the six through nine age range is the nature of evening television programming. Youngsters of this age are ill-equipped to deal with the stark boldness, the negative values, aggressiveness, and sex on television each night.

A direct way to curtail a prominent family-breaker such as television viewing is by restricting viewing for those in this age range. Certainly, there are evening television programs that are worthwhile, and exceptions can be made. The reader can refer to the chart concerning bedtimes for this age range.

Naps and Sleeping Habits

The child between six and nine will nap in the daytime only infrequently. Parents should be alert to excessive tiredness and irritability that may be due to fatigue and ask the child if he or she would like to take a "rest." The word "nap" should be avoided because many children associate it with infants. A child who might rest comfortably may nap reluctantly. If the child insists on excessive rest during this age (particularly for the eight- and nine-year-old), consultation with the pediatrician should be made.

Occasionally, a child of this age will request to sleep with a parent. This is considerably more common among children younger than five, but it may persist for older children. In general, children who are older than six should not sleep with their parents and should be discouraged from doing so. If the child is insistent and the parent cannot convince him or her to sleep independently, a reasonable compromise is for the parent to sleep in the child's bed rather than the child sleeping in the parent's bed. The parent can then wean gradually away from the child's bed by leaving at progressively earlier times on successive nights. Occasionally, a child will wander into the parents's bedroom during the night, while the parents are asleep, and will be found curled up at the foot of the bed in the morning. This behavior should also be discouraged.

Of course, there are reasonable exceptions to the rule. When out-of-town guests stay in the home, for example, and it becomes logical for the parents to sleep with a child, or when the family is traveling and has limited sleeping space in motels.

Bed-Wetting

In this age range, bed-wetting should not be considered a psychological problem. If it occurs frequently the parents should check with a pediatrician to determine if infections or physical problems might be the cause.

In our experience, the primary problems caused by nightly bed-wetting are social and limit or prevent the child from visiting other children, camping, or having other children spend the night. If bed-wetting is a problem, the child should be helped because of the social stigma as well as the additional work and inconvenience for the parent.

A child can be helped in several ways. Liquids should be restricted after 6:00 P.M., and the child should be rewarded for using the toilet before bedtime. If these efforts are embarrassing to the youngster, it can be done separately from the family and with a relative degree of privacy. The parents might make a determination concerning when the wetting usually takes place and wake the child before then. Also, one parent might wake the child to use the bathroom several hours after the child falls asleep.

Often, a simple drawing of a person that shows a light bulb going on in the head area and its connection to the genital area will help the child to see the relationship and to realize when he or she has to use the bathroom. A device is available that we have found extremely effective in curtailing or terminating bed-wetting. The device is a sheet that contains a buzzer that is activated when the child begins to urinate. The child is awakened and can use the bathroom before total voiding occurs. This is not foolproof, however. A youngster may be an extremely heavy sleeper, and everyone in the house may be awakened by the buzzer but the child.

An eight- or nine-year-old bed-wetter can also be reminded of the inappropriateness of this behavior by being responsible for cleaning the wet sheets.

Whining and Fussing

Whining and idle fussing frequently occur in this age range and take on a greater degree of sophistication than in the three to five year age range, both in terms of the type of fussing and the reasons. It must be determined if the child needs help or protection or if the whining is a means of getting attention. If a child is trying to gain attention, he or she should be ignored initially and, if the behavior persists, punished.

Parents should be aware of the time of day that whining occurs. If it occurs around dinner time, for example, the child may simply be indicating hunger. In fact, the child may even deny being hungry. If whining occurs around bedtime or in the early evening hours, there is a strong likelihood that the youngster is tired. Parents should make a strenuous effort to control their negative responses toward a whining child, if the whining is occurring because of such basic physiological needs as hunger or fatigue.

The same considerations and approach in general should be taken at this age level for whining and fussing as in the three to five year age group. (See Chapter 6.) After the age of seven, however, the reward of stars alone for proper behavior are usually not sufficient encouragement for the child to change the behavior. Also, the child may feel the stars are a bit "babyish," and it may be advisable to use checks, stamps, or other marks on a chart, if a chart is used. In addition, there are different sets of positive behaviors related to the self-esteem of a child at this age than of a younger one.

There are many more social rewards that can be granted or withheld at this point, such as staying up later at night, parents spending more time reading a story at night, and others that can be incentives to reduce whining.

If whining takes place on Sunday night and is associated with complaints about work at school, or if there have been any problems in the child's handwriting, reading, or listening skills in school, the complaining may be a clue that the child is not happy in school. A child at this age may have some limited insight into what is making him unhappy, and this should be explored by the parent. However, if the child's explanation does not make sense or if it does not lead to a solution, lengthy reasoning sessions should be avoided.

Temper Tantrums

Temper tantrums in this age range are rare. If a child has frequent temper tantrums, parents should strongly consider a medical examination for the child to determine if there is a physical reason for such behavior. If a physician reports that the child is healthy, parents should then closely look at their behavior in response to the child's temper tantrums.

If mother or father gives in to the youngster or provides unusual attention (even negative attention) for temper tantrums, the child may misbehave to achieve specific objectives or to gain the "reward" of parental attention.

We have found the "time-out" procedure very effective in dealing with temper tantrums at this age. The child is put into his or her room (or if that is too stimulating, which is often the case, a less attractive room) for a period of time to calm down. Some thirty seconds to three minutes after the child has calmed, the child is permitted to leave the room. During the time-out, the youngster should be alone, unless the parents are concerned that the child may get hurt.

Another approach is for the parent to record marks on a chart for misbehavior and to ignore the child during the tantrum. When a certain number of marks are accumulated, the child loses a major privilege. Just ignoring the tantrum may not work, however, especially if others are involved and the child is rewarded by their negative attention. The authors are reminded of a youngster who cleared a large food store of people by throwing a temper tantrum that the mother stoically ignored.

Self-Inflicted Injuries

Children who hurt themselves are even more rare at this age than those who throw temper tantrums. Unless there is a severe emotional problem, which is even more rare, this type of self-inflicted injury should be dealt with in the same way that temper tantrums are dealt with. The child may be seriously injured, however, and more active restraint might be needed if parents become concerned for the child's safety.

Fears

There are many reasons for fear in this age range, especially in connection with the demands and expectations placed on the child by parents, peers, school, and society. Although the development of fears is perfectly normal, excessive fears should be scrutinized. What is the child afraid of? Is the parent contributing to the fear by discussing the issue excessively, or rewarding the fear in other ways?

The parent is caught in the curious conflict of not wanting to reward fear, yet not wanting the child to feel forsaken if the parent ignores the behavior. For the eight- or nine-year-old, and often for the six- and seven-year-old, clear intellectual discussions concerning the irrationality of the fear often are successful. Parents should remember that they can experiment with approaches to the child's fear. No permanent damage will be done to a child if parental efforts to ignore the fear extend over several days or even to two weeks. Frequently, we see fears disappear or become extremely diluted when they are ignored by parents for a week or two.

Occasionally, the child hesitates or is resistant about attending school at this age, and this often comes out as a fear. This could be either resistance to attending school or resistance to leaving home. Close coordination with the teacher, or at least information from the teacher about the child's behavior and response at school, is called for. Behavior modification can be used to treat school fears if it is determined that there are no definable causes of the fear at school, such as extreme aggressiveness by another child.

Often, children with subtle specific learning disabilities are afraid of school. Discussion among parent, teacher, and child should take place to determine if this is the case. Often the subtleness of such developmental lag makes its discovery extremely difficult; it is obscured not only from the child and parent but also from the teacher.

In regard to school fears where clear factors—such as overly aggressive classmates or a harried teacher—cannot be determined, parental calmness, directness, firmness, and perhaps a good behavioral program will probably solve the problem.

Allowance

The child in the six to nine age range should receive an allowance on a particular day every week. A percentage of the money received should be awarded "free" to the child for simply being a member of the family. However, a percentage of the allowance should also be provided for successful attempts and completion of assigned responsibilities and chores. As the youngster grows older and the amount of money provided through allowances increase, the percentage of money earned through successful participation and responsibilities and chores should be increased.

Some creative use of the allowance can be used to particularly good advantage in this age range. For example, a bonus or a percentage of the allowance can be provided if a child, who might be having difficulty getting along with a sibling, spends time in peaceful coexistence. In this regard, it is wise to break down the time periods so that the reward is given for small periods of time, such as half days, or even hours, instead of full weeks.

For example, twenty-eight cents of a child's allowance could be given for fourteen half days per week in which the child did not fight, the rate being two cents per half day. Of course, two failures, that is two half days in which fighting did occur, would result in only twenty-four cents for the week based on the same schedule. The chart in Chapter 2 shows the approximate amount of allowance that a child of this age should receive.

Responsibilities

Responsibilities given to children in this age range are of considerable importance. Recognition of the child's role, importance, and responsibility within the family, and to the family members, can be taught through assigned household responsibilities.

In farm and rural families, children from about age six begin to assume important responsibilities in the family. They carry their load, become *contributors* and, therefore, important to the family.

The child raised in the city, on the other hand, is usually a *consumer* of family resources rather than a contributor and can easily become a burden to his parents. The importance of meaningful chores and responsibilities for children of urban families is clearer in the context of this information.

Chores, or responsibilities, assigned should be of two basic types: responsibility for management of the child's own room or areas; responsibility for the completion of a chore upon which the rest of the family depends.

In regard to the first category, such responsibilities as making one's bed, cleaning one's room, or shining one's shoes are applicable. As with many other issues, it is important that the youngster is not charged with responsibilities that he or she cannot perform. An error here will obviously result in mutual resentment.

In regard to the second category, the family has tasks such as garbage removal, retrieving garbage cans, assisting with yard work, retrieving the newspaper, and in general those chores or responsibilities that affect the family directly.

In addition to being cautious about not giving the child in this age range responsibilities that the child cannot perform (such as cutting the grass), it should be remembered that the skill level of a child of seven or eight is far below that of a ten- or eleven-year-old. Completion, not perfection, should be the goal, and it should be rewarded.

A child should be rewarded for appropriate discharge of responsibilities, and approximations of success, much the same way as adults are rewarded for their efforts. Do not hesitate to express pleasure with the child's performance and make a portion of an allowance contingent upon a child's efforts. Do not believe the somewhat popular myth that children (or people in general, strangely enough) should never be rewarded for "behavior that simply is expected." Adults are usually rewarded (monetarily, socially, etc.) for any behavior they have performed. This is true for activities such as employment and chores at home and other responsibilities that adults perform that are not especially attractive. Children should be rewarded also.

The following suggestions for housework may be used as regular responsibilities performed without pay or as additional sources of income for the child.

Table 6. Job and Salary Chart

Job	Salary
Water lawn or plants (for ten minutes)	$.05
Feed dog	.05
Give dog water	.05
Straighten up house (empty ashtrays, throw away paper, put away toys, shoes, other belongings)	.15
Set table	.05
Clean bedroom (put away toys, pick up clothes)	.10
Clean closet (hang up clothes, throw out junk, put away toys)	.15
Make bed (not perfectly)	.05
Dust furniture	.10
Wash car on outside	.50
Sweep porch (small porch)	.05

Discipline

Discipline is vital. Our years of professional and personal experience with families have made it clear to us that children react positively to parents who make demands on them and insist that they become better than they are. Without a clear conception of what type of citizen a child should strive to become, that child is unlikely to show cooperation, commitment, or self-discipline.

The child who is dealt with in an overly permissive fashion is given too much power in the family and an insufficient amount of limits and direction. The youngster who is dealt with by a parent who is overly permissive tends to be a fearful child because of the amount of power that he or she wields. In addition, such a child often shows little respect for institutions, goals, or self-discipline.

The overprotected child also receives insufficient discipline as the parents try to protect the child from malevolent forces. Certainly the child who is not yet a teenager needs to be protected from the erosion of morals and values. The nine-year-old, however, should begin to be exposed, at least in conversations, to factors for which protection has been provided previously. We find that children who are overprotected experience difficulty in social judgment as they grow older and show an excessive degree of idealism and naïveté.

In the six to nine age range, transgressions should be punished. Wise parents, however, also deal with successful behavior through reward. Both are clearly forms of discipline, one stressing the positive and the other the negative.

Too much punishment can tend to alienate a child. This certainly reduces a parent's ability to influence a child. Punishments such as reasonable removal of privileges, restriction to room or house, removal of bicycle, restrictions on television-viewing, and requiring additional chores are all reasonable. Parents should remember that a child will not dislike them for punishment, and parents should not hesitate to punish when punishment is due.

Sincere caution must be exercised by the parent, who should realize that the child's recognition of time is considerably different than an adult's. Two or three days of punishment typically suffice to modify behavior for a serious, persistent, and intentional negative pattern. A two-week restriction for a child in this age range is an *extremely* severe punishment. If a restriction extends beyond two or three days, we often find that children forget why they are being punished and that resentment is building toward their parents.

Spanking a child in this age range is often an effective punishment but there are individual differences in children. Parents may spank their children if their behavior endangers themselves or others, or if it is potentially destructive.

Parents should observe the consequences of spanking on a child's behavior. If the behavior for which the child is being spanked persists, then the spanking is ineffective and should be terminated. Continued spanking that does not curtail the activity for which it is applied can make a child angry and resentful.

To aid in adding structure and control, as well as increasing responsibility in a child of this age, the reader is referred to Chapter 5.

Divorce

Divorce to a child in this age range is frequently a traumatic experience in which a beloved parent leaves the home. The amount of explanation given the child for the split should be contingent on how volatile the parent's behavior has been, how much the child realizes anyway, and the child's feelings toward the departing parent.

Divorce may cause a child not only to feel helpless and confused, but also guilty. It should be explained to the child that he or she is not to blame and that both parents still love the child. Visitation with the absent parent should occur as frequently as possible, providing this departing parent is not a negative influence. The parents should not criticize each other in the presence of the child.

The courts, often with professional assistance, must determine visitations. We have seen a child testify against a parent in court, and we find this to be an extremely damaging experience for the child—regardless of age. If possible, this should *never* occur to any youngster, and lawyers should be discouraged from "using" a child in this way.

We recommend several references for children whose parents are being divorced. These books are appropriate for children between the ages of eight and fourteen. We have found the following books to be effective: *The Boys' and Girls' Book about Divorce* by Richard A. Gardner, M.D., and *Where Is Daddy? The Story of a Divorce* by Beth Goff.

While parents should not go into the sordid details regarding their ex-mates, especially in an attempt to blame the other partner for the divorce, this does not mean that the whole issue should be presented to the child as a mystery. Even though the parent probably does not completely understand why the divorce took place— all the hidden, subtle, and subconscious patterns that have resulted in the divorce—the parent may be able to describe the reasons for the divorce in general.

A woman might say: "Your father spent too much time at his

business and was often at meetings in the evening so that I did not feel I could count on him in a crisis and did not feel this gave us enough time to talk."

Or: "Your father feels that I spent too much time in social club work. I did spend a great deal of time outside of the home, but I believe this was to make up for the lack of time that I had with your father and to provide me with someone to talk with and express my feelings to."

Or a man might say: "Your mother and I have grown apart. My work keeps me so busy and our interests grew apart so that we have little in common."

Sometimes children pretend that they have no feelings regarding the divorce, but they are probably just hiding them. This is not healthy, and the child should be encouraged to discuss happy, sad, angry, and frustrating feelings related to the parents and the divorce. Sometimes children feel they are to blame for the divorce and that it resulted because their bad behavior upset their parents. Although children's behavior is not the best at times (and often is particularly poor immediately preceding a separation or divorce because of the stress on the child), the child must be made to see that every child behaves badly at times and that this had nothing to do with the divorce.

Conversely, the child should not attempt to be perfect as a way of making up for previous bad behavior or as an attempt to bring the parents back together. The child should be made to understand that both parents still exist, even though the divorce has taken place, and that the divorce does not mean that the child has lost a parent. Children should not feel that they are responsible for replacing the missing parent, either in terms of responsibilities or affection. The child may need to take on some more responsibilities to help a parent but the child cannot be a substitute mother or father. The parents still need to find much of their affection and communication with other adults, just as they did when the family lived together.

Although a fairly rigid visitation schedule should be set up during the first six months after a divorce to provide security for the child, after this time the youngster should not be required to visit with the parent who is not living in the home if some other truly legitimate activity arises. If possible, the child should speak directly to the visiting parent to set up a substitute time.

Children should *never* be used to inform on the other parent and describe the other parent's relationships with dates, stepmothers, or stepfathers. Parents should not attempt to have their child take sides. The child may acquire too much responsibility and power and eventually play one parent against the other. The child should understand that he or she can show affection and interest in a stepparent and that this does not mean that interest or love in the natural parent must be given up.

Death and Funerals

When death occurs in a family, it is difficult for everyone concerned, but particularly for a child in the six to nine year age range. At this age, children have only a vague understanding of death, and frequently experience fears about death. The circumstance under which the death has taken place should typically determine what action is taken with the child. Communication should be made directly, honestly, and privately to permit the immediate release of emotions in an unencumbered and uninhibited fashion. If a death has taken place under particularly unpleasant circumstances, these details should be neglected in discussing the death with the child. The use of statements such as, "He is in heaven," are quite helpful to a child in this age range.

As a general rule of thumb, children up to the age of nine or ten should not view the body. Seeing the deceased loved one does not provide the same possible cathartic experience as it does for an adult. Often children are bewildered and greatly confused by the events and the emotionalism shown at funerals. Attendance at a religious service, assuming closed casket, and burial is sufficient reality for the child.

In general, children should stay close to home until major crises pass. Such crises include a parent's illness, a death in the family, a neighborhood upheaval, or a problem with relatives or friends.

The child should stay close to home, close to parents, and communication should flow between parent and child at these times. When the storm is over, the child can resume normal activities.

Intellectual Slowness

The retarded child in the six to nine age range will show generally broad gaps or substantial developmental lags across all areas of intellectual, academic, and, frequently, social and physical development. If the retarded child is not detected as a preschooler, he or she will frequently enter a classroom situation that is entirely too difficult, and a great deal of frustration may occur. Professional evaluation and proper placement is entirely in order for any child if parents—after consultation with a trusted professional such as a pediatrician—believe the child might be retarded.

Hyperactivity

Frequently hyperactive children are tolerated by their parents before they enter school. When such children enter school, however, the parents may receive a frantic call from an exhausted and dismayed classroom teacher, who is attempting to control a classroom in the face of the poor attention span of a hyperactive six-year-old.

The hyperactive six-year-old will not become active under certain circumstances, often showing long minutes of attention to cherished activities or events. But when placed in a highly stimulating environment, hyperactivity occurs. We have come to call this type of response "hyper-reactivity."

Of significance here is medication that pediatricians can prescribe for hyperactivity. The parents of a hyperactive child should definitely consult a pediatrician.

With the hyperactive child, we have found a higher incidence of learning disability, and the parents should be alert for this possibility.

The hyperactive child should not be placed in an "open" classroom because an excessive amount of stimulation is present.

Parent-Child Time

Remember, one-to-one time between parent and child is necessary for the child's proper development and represents the closest thing known to a "cure-all" in terms of preventing and solving family problems.

As with the three- to five-year-old, ideally, the father and mother should spend at least two twenty-minute periods per week with (1) each child (2) in total or semi-isolation from other siblings (3) doing something the child enjoys (and, preferably, that the parent enjoys somewhat), (4) which is not goal-oriented or perfectionistic or competitive, (5) where oftentimes the parent is in a guiding but absolutely nonjudgmental or critical role (if the child builds a model and puts the wheels on the roof this is excellent because it gives the parent an opportunity to demonstrate that the *only* goal of their time together is to have fun and enjoy each other.) (6) This time is in addition to any other time spent with the child that does not meet these five criteria.

Achievements and aspirations will be instilled during parent-child contacts. They are as important in the development of goals and values as home responsibilities, work experiences, and good school and good peer influences.

School

Six-year-olds enter school with unequalled eagerness to learn to read and may be disappointed if they do not learn to read the first day. Normally during the first school year, children will learn to recognize letters and will accumulate approximately two hundred words. They will be able to recall words by sight and learn to associate sounds and written symbols.

Seven-year-olds should be able to use sounds of initial consonants, consonant blends such as *bl, br, sp, sc,* and ending consonants. They should also be able to distinguish between words and read short unfamiliar words.

Eight-year-olds will be able to read approximately nine hundred words. They will learn to use clues such as short and long vowels, consonants, vowel diagraphs (two letters that make one sound), and vowel diphthongs (*oi, oy,* for example) to recognize new words. In addition, they should be instructed in the basic rules of syllabication, and they will be taught basic prefixes and suffixes.

It is not unusual for six-year-olds to reverse letters such as *b* for *d* or *p* for *q*. They may even reverse words: *on* for *no, was* for *saw*. They might rotate letters: *b* for *g* or *d* for *p*. However, if this confusion continues to the age of seven or eight, it may indicate an inability to distinguish left from right.

If the child cannot project directions from his body into space, such as right and left, up and down, by the age of seven, the following exercises may help.

Play the game of "You Must." In playing this game the parent says for example, "You must touch your right hand to your left ear," or "Touch your right elbow with your left hand." This game should be played until the child's responses increase in speed and accuracy to the point that they become automatic. When the child has mastered "You Must," games using a flashlight may begin. For example, the child faces a wall while the parent shines the beam of light on the wall at eye level. The beam moves slowly from the right to the left, left to right, up to down, down to up, as the child states the direction in which the light is moving. After this game has been mastered, the light can be flashed directly on the child's body. The child then states which part of the body the light is shining on—right shoulder, left knee, left hand.

At this point, the child should be ready to apply this skill to pencil and paper. On a large piece of paper, the child should draw a square starting in the left top corner, reporting the direction of the movement as it is made. If a child has difficulty with this particular task, he or she can do it physically first by hopping, walking, or skipping the shape of a square, verbalizing the changes in direction.

Another difficulty occurs when there is recognition of a word on one line and several lines later the child might be unable to call that same word. This child is probably not playing games or being obstinate: he or she really cannot recognize that word because it is in a different word grouping. The child gets an entirely different visual stimulus when the word is surrounded by a different set of words. This problem is often described as a "figure-ground deficit." It will seem to some children with this problem that their eyes are jumping all over the page and not focusing on the one word they are trying to read.

A window card will be helpful to the child with this difficulty.

The card is simply a three-by-five-inch, plain index card with a slot, or window, cut in it to show only one word at a time. As the child reads, he or she moves the card along, and it shows only one word at a time. As the child learns to focus on the one word, a larger window card may be made to show three or four words, or a short phrase. Eventually, a window card that shows a complete line can be used.

Another problem occurring with children at this age is the inability to read an entire word. The child may attack the word only by its first letter, for example, reading "aunt" as "apple." Practice in matching lists of words with their appropriate "frames" is often helpful in overcoming this difficulty. Figure 4 shows some samples of words and frames.

There is another group of children who seem to have a great deal of difficulty mastering basic words, such as "was," which are taught by sight rather than by sounding out. This learning problem may be due to a deficit in visual memory. An activity that can help improve visual memory is for a child to reproduce colored block designs after exposure of two seconds per block, or reproduce bead designs from memory after a two second exposure per bead in the pattern. Some suggested block or bead patterns are blue cube, red ball, yellow ball, green cube. A more complex presentation could consist of small blue cube, large red ball, large green cube, small yellow cylinder, small red ball. Start with a small number and gradually increase as the child becomes more proficient.

Simple patterns may be followed by more involved ones that can be purchased from Teaching Resources, 100 Boylston Street, Boston, Massachusetts 02116, and Developmental Learning Materials, 7440 Natchez Avenue, Niles, Illinois 60648.

A next step is the use of parquetry blocks and designs, which can be purchased from Developmental Learning Materials. Parquetry blocks are shaped as squares, triangles, diamonds, and half diamonds. Pattern cards are presented to the child whose task is to reproduce the pattern by properly combining the different shaped blocks.

Another activity that will improve visual memory is displaying

Figure 4. Word Frames

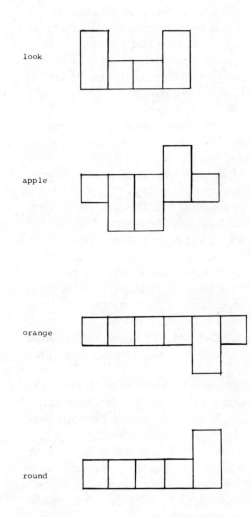

a number of objects on a tray for one second per object, then covering the tray and having the child name as many objects as possible. The number of objects on the tray should be low enough to ensure success initially. The number can be gradually increased.

When the seven-year-old is able to remember eight to ten objects, the objects can be placed in a definite sequence and both the objects and the proper sequence asked of the child. When initiating this phase, the number of objects should be decreased initially and then gradually increased.

Many children will become proficient in naming objects in sequence but be unable to generalize this skill to letters. The parent can expose a card with a series of letters, starting with two at one second per letter, then covering the card and having the child name and write the letters in sequence from left to right. It is important that the letters be written as well as spoken.

Many children have difficulty correlating letters, or letter combinations, with the sounds they represent. If phonics training has been adequate, this may be due to an "auditory discrimination" problem. If a child needs help in this skill, exercises should be started to develop "same or different" concepts. These exercises should start with the parent reading pairs of words where some of the initial sounds are changed. Next, word pairs should be practiced with the middle sounds changed. The last step in the word pairs is to change the final sound. Table 7 lists some examples.

Table 7. Word Pairs

Initial	*Medial*	*Final*
bit-pit	trip-trap	his-hit
yet-yet	pen-pan	bit-big
pig-rig	sit-sit	lean-lead
ledge-ledge	sill-sale	blue-blue
call-tall	sleek-slick	presence-present
pig-dig	woke-wake	stance-stand
darn-barn	vine-vine	third-thirst
bolster-bolster	bean-been	save-same
night-might	steam-stem	cloud-cloud
jog-bog	more-more	leave-leaf

When a consistent level of proficiency is reached, exercises should proceed to phrases and then complete sentences. (See Table 8.)

Table 8.   Phrase and Sentence Pairs

Phrases

Your brother—your mother
All night—all right
Must go—must know
The yellow ball—the yellow ball
Has found—has ground
When I wash—when I wish
From the farm—from the farm
What I want—what I want
You will chew—You will do
The white duck—the white duck

Sentences

Begin eating.   Begin beating.
Is he sitting?   Is he hitting?
Where are the posts?   Where are the ghosts?
It is beautiful countryside.   It is beautiful countryside.
He will not admit it.   He will not admit it.
That is a habit.   That is a rabbit.
He walked down the hill.   He walked down the hill.
The road began to wind.   The road began to wind.
It is best to eat slowly.   It is best to heat slowly.
It is the center of the tin industry.   It is the center of the pin industry.

The child should not be looking at the person saying the words or phrases because the child will receive visual clues.

Perhaps parents have heard comments from teachers or read them on report cards that indicate the child "daydreams," "doesn't pay attention," or "is inattentive." Too often, these observations signal a deficit in the auditory avenue of learning but are incorrectly treated, as behavior problems.

The child's deficit may be an inability to follow verbal directions, to store what is heard for future use, or to mentally close up and understand a word that the child has only heard parts of.

A deficit in "auditory closure," which is what this deficiency is called, may cause the child to misinterpret verbal directions or instructions. To develop this skill, words with parts left out should be said to a child. The child should then say the complete word such as: __olli__op (lollipop); ice __ream __one (ice cream cone); —ellybean (jellybean); —or— and —uggy (horse and buggy).

To develop auditory memory, first start with verbal instructions that have one step, then move to two steps, three steps, and four steps. Examples of the various levels are listed in Table 9.

Table 9.   Auditory Memory Exercises: Commands

One step

point to your nose
place your hand on your head
remove one book from the shelf
skip around your chair twice
hop on your right foot three times

Two steps

walk to the wall; now come back here
point to the window; then show me a book
run to the door; then sit on the floor
snap your fingers; then touch your knee
turn your chair around; and then stand behind it

Three steps

raise your hand; then say your name; then wave good-bye
first, raise your arms up straight; then jump up and down;
      then try to touch your nose
bring me the blue crayola; then touch your knees;
      then hop on your right foot
tap your foot; then clap your hands; then do both together
tell me the name of your neighbor; hop three times on your right foot;
      and then point to your eyes.

Four steps

point to the left; then point to the right; next you turn around, and
    then you touch the ground.
put your hands on your head; then pick up the book; then fold the
    paper; then walk to the door.
walk sideways to the front of the room; then sit down; and put your
    hands on your knees; and, finally, walk back and forth.
make your arms into a circle; make a triangle with the fingers of both
    hands; then stretch your arms up toward the sky; and then
    show me how to swim.
bow your head; then cover your ears; then put your hands on your
    waist and then jump up and down four times.

After a child can follow these types of verbal instructions, the
parent can introduce memory for unrelated words. This area
should start with two words and build to four or five words, adding one word at a time as each level is mastered. If the child appears to have mastered one level but is unable to perform the next
level without frustration, the parent should review the previous
level. Table 10 lists word sequences.

Table 10.   Auditory Memory Exercises: Unrelated Words

List #1

shape—dried
sounds—animals
color—such
look—themselves
words—toy
interest—play
storybooks—used
five—colored
show—children
repeat—animals

List #2

pale—prayer—brave
flies—limb—grow
dwarf—flow—act
sew—queer—have

broke—patch—twin
kite—plan—gum
chop—pine—tale
trick—gas—melt
where—chalk—squeak
drew—stuck—miss

List #3

words—build—child—should
hand—thumb—walk—pick
show—master—then—flies
waste—neighbor—book—fast
three—bump—witch—light
tool—hatch—waste—move
appear—care—sneeze—word
times—sing—different—game
dress—great—quickly—mixed
worry—might—well—tight

After the memory for unrelated words has been performed, the child should be ready to attempt memory for related words or sentences. Like the unrelated words, the sentences should start with only two words and progress one word at a time until there are eight or ten words in a sentence. Some examples of the type of sentences that can be used are listed in Table 11.

Most children find writing an easily developed skill; however, many find learning to write a monumental task. They cannot seem to control the pencil or form the letters correctly in a relaxed manner and may be described in school as lazy or unwilling to complete their work. There are two primary causes for this difficulty: underdeveloped eye-to-hand coordination or underdeveloped fine muscle control.

Manipulating clay into objects and working with fingerpaints will help develop the fine muscle strength and control necessary for writing. Individual fingers may be strengthened by taking clothespins off and placing them on a piece of rope. The child should grasp the spring-type clothespin with the thumb and one finger at a time. The palm of the hand should be downward with the thumb at the bottom so that the thumb and the fingers are

Table 11.   Auditory Memory Exercises: Related Words

Go home.
Jump up.
March now.
Who's here?
Leaf is green.
The elephant danced.
Simon says run.
The moon shines.
The monkey is funny.
A water rate increase.
Stand there and wave.
Three more stars showed.
Mr. Owl has slanted eyes.
The bus always slows down.
Thanksgiving is for eating turkey.
Dancer and Prancer are reindeers.
The ant hill was very high.
Animals in the zoo are interesting.
The pink elephant's name was Dumbo.
Boats were sailing into the sunset.
The beetle was crawling across the ground.
The tooth fairy visited me last night.
The storm was raging in the sky.
The baseball player made a home run.
Brothers and sisters do not always play together.
Giraffes have very long legs and a long neck.
The Green Giant is a make-believe fellow.
Baseball teams have nine players on each side.
The lion cubs sounded and played just like kittens.
In England's Whipsnade Zoo, the lions roam the grounds.
The State Fair is a once a year occasion.
Jose Gaspar sailed up the river to conquer Tampa.
Ring around the rosy is a game all children play.
At length, I found myself under a tree tangled up.
The tidal waves rose high as the wind blew briskly.
The wind was blowing strong and the snow was high.

working like pincers. The index and middle fingers are the important ones to strengthen in order to develop better writing.

Until fine muscle control is developed, children should not be encouraged to write small or even normal-size letters. Some chil-

Figure 5.   Writing Movements

1.
   A.   .A

   B.   .B

   C.   .C

   D.   .D

2.
  A **B** **C** **D**

  A **B** **C** **D**

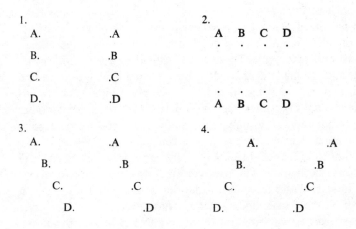

3.
   A.   .A

    B.   .B

     C.   .C

      D.   .D

4.
     A.   .A

    B.   .B

   C.   .C

  D.   .D

5.

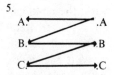

6.

7.

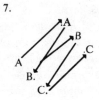

167

dren may need to be encouraged to write letters as large as two or three inches.

To aid the development of "near-point" eye-to-hand coordination, the child can trace and cut geometric forms such as circles, squares, and rectangles. These forms should be five to six inches in size and gradually decreased. After the child is able to trace and cut these forms, staying on the lines, simple figures such as airplanes, houses, or other familiar objects can be used. Another activity that children usually enjoy and that is good for near-point coordination is connecting dots to form pictures.

If the child has a blackboard, the exercises described here could also be helpful. The procedure in these exercises is for the child to start with the chalk on the dot at one letter and stop at the dot on the corresponding letter. These exercises are for practicing strokes in various directions, left to right, top to bottom, which simulate the strokes used in writing. (See Figure 5.)

As an aid to and a preparation for academic work, the child can trace large letters (perhaps beaded ones) with a finger, then with a pencil or crayon. If problems developing this skill persist, the child may write in bird tray gravel or sand with the index finger. (Bird tray gravel is easier to work with and easier to brush off hands.)

To develop gross motor or "far-point" eye-to-hand coordination, such activities as beanbag or ring toss, or horseshoes are beneficial. In any one of these activities, initially the child should be close to the target, perhaps a foot or two away. As proficiency develops, the child can move back a foot or two at a time.

If a child has difficulty moving from one level to another or continues to have difficulty with academic tasks, it is probable that a specific learning disability is the cause. A complete medical evaluation should be scheduled with a pediatrician. Referral should be made to a licensed psychologist and an experienced specialist in learning disabilities who will work together with the child.

8 The Pre-Teen

This period can be a comfortable time for both the child and the parent. It certainly tends to be less stormy than the thirteen to fifteen age range. By age ten children are able to care for themselves in many respects and do not require as much control and attention in terms of dressing, eating, and other such day-to-day activities.

Children will develop broader social contacts during this period and may be permitted to ride their bicycles many blocks from home depending upon traffic conditions. They may run with a neighborhood "gang," although they should not be allowed to stay out for more than two hours at age ten without checking back at home, and no longer than three hours in the eleven to twelve range. Other outside groups include Scouting, Little League baseball activities, day camp, and even overnight summer camp.

Children at this age should develop many interests, such as reading for pleasure, model building, other arts and crafts, baseball, basketball, bowling, ballet, baton lessons, crocheting, cooking, embroidery, knitting, sewing, card games, board games, field trips, fishing, and swimming. Competitive football and hockey are generally not advisable for this age because of potential injury to growing bodies.

Sex Education

Boys and girls should now be given the biological facts about sex if they have not asked questions before the age of ten. Most children will not have asked sufficient questions regarding sex and, of course, a girl will need to be instructed about menstruation. This sexual instruction should be simple, brief, and straightforward.

First, it is necessary to have a vocabulary so that specific instruction can take place. Terms such as "penis," "vagina," and "uterus" may be used to explain that the seed is planted by placing the penis into the vagina, that this is what parents do to have children, and that this is an enjoyable experience that parents share. The development of the fetus in the uterus and the eventual birth can all be discussed briefly with the entire instruction usually taking no more than fifteen to thirty minutes.

Children should be instructed privately by their parents and much should be made of the fact that they are now old enough and smart enough to share in this information, which their older brothers and sisters already possess. Parents can also use pencil and paper to draw the penis and vagina. While this may be awkward or embarrassing to the parents, they should forge ahead anyway with the explanation.

Children at this age are certainly curious about their own bodies and those of the opposite sex. Self-exploration and exploration of others should not be shocking to adults. The eleven- or twelve-year-old is getting beyond the point of "playing doctor," however, and exploration should be stopped with a simple statement such as, "We don't do that."

Sometimes children in this age range touch their genitals in the classroom or at home. Usually this can be curtailed if the parent quietly, firmly, and calmly brings this behavior to the child's attention. In the classroom, the child can be told to go to the bathroom when the behavior occurs. Usually the novelty will wear off rapidly.

Obscene Language

Ten- and eleven-year-old children who use gutter language, curse, or write dirty words are probably attempting to gain attention for themselves and do not actually know the meanings of some of the words they use. But they do know these are taboo words.

Since the child may be looking for a reaction, parents must not overreact, but simply tell their children that these are not proper words to be written or spoken, especially with the family. If they continue then points can be deducted from a behavior chart to reduce privileges for each statement. (Follow the problem-solving formula of Chapter 4.)

Parents should realize that if they use this kind of language then their children are likely to do so also. This does not mean that a parent should tell a child that it is all right to use this language if the parent does, but it certainly makes it difficult to teach the child if the parents are setting a negative example.

Bragging

Children at this age often have a tendency to brag about themselves and build themselves up in games and athletic competition. They may even cheat at games, especially if there are older siblings the child feels in competition with. Parents and older siblings must try to refrain from pointing out to the child that he or she is not capable even when they are sure the child is not. They should give the child an opportunity to accomplish things whenever possible and reflect the child's feelings by saying "I guess you sure would like to win that game," or "You feel you are even better than your father at that."

Sometimes bragging reflects too much emphasis on competition and perfectionism in the family. Parents should spend more time with their children developing relationships around activities that are not based on perfection.

Some children at this age will give away their allowance to friends or purchase items to give away to friends in school or in the neighborhood. This is usually an attempt to "buy" friends, and children should not be bailed out when the allowance runs out. At the same time, parents must help to build the child's ego academically, socially, or athletically and encourage the child to develop one or two good friendships in which "prostitution" is not involved.

Guns, Knives, and Matches

A few children at this age will be fascinated by guns, knives, and matches. Such curiosity is natural and does not indicate that the child will turn out to be an assassin or arsonist. It is perhaps heightened by an interest of the parents, such as collecting guns, or a vicarious influence of the media.

Often this interest can be channeled so the child learns proper control of these areas. For example, children might be asked to light Father's pipe or use matches in appropriate social ways. They might be asked to help prepare meals by cutting with a knife. Or, they might be enrolled in a riflery course at a police rifle range where they will be taught gun safety.

Responsibilities

The ten-, eleven-, and twelve-year-old could benefit from three home responsibilities a day in addition to one half hour of work per week at a pay schedule as follows: thirty cents per hour for the ten-year-old, thirty-five cents per hour for the eleven-year-old, and forty cents per hour for the twelve-year-old. These responsibilities could include such tasks as emptying the garbage from the house into an outside container or from many small containers into one large container. It could include removing dishes from the table, setting the table, making the bed, and cleaning up personal rooms. At this age level, room cleaning should include hanging clothes on hangers and even sweeping with a vacuum cleaner.

Children should set their own alarm clocks to awaken for school. They should dress themselves, although clothes may still be laid out the night before or in the morning for the younger child. The ten- or eleven-year-old should be able to handle all of this alone. Certainly, children of this age should be expected to pour their own juice and prepare their own breakfast cereal.

In addition, the child in this age range might be asked by his parents to participate in special projects, such as painting a fence or yard work. This could be on a pay schedule, or if it is only occasionally, the child could be asked to do this as part of his or her contribution to the family.

Whereas eight- and nine-year-olds are not sufficiently mature to use a power driven lawn mower, edger, or other power equipment, ten- and eleven-year-olds may be able to assume these kinds of responsibilities. But parents may need to supervise and to offer reminders of the dangers involved. Special care should be taken that the child does not use such a responsibility as a game or to show off in front of his peers.

Both sexes should be given an opportunity to work at most tasks. Men often make outstanding chefs, and male soldiers are required to make their own beds and to be "kitchen police." Girls should be given the opportunity to engage in aggressive and assertive chores requiring physical exertion or mechanical problem-solving.

The child of this age still needs an occasional reminder to do work because he or she will forget the time. Whenever possible, responsibilities should be set for a time of the day that will make it easy for the youngster to remember the prescribed tasks. For example, setting the table for dinner has an automatic reminder built into it. Other activities can be timed to take place before dinner, before noon on Saturday, at times preceding play, watching television, or other pleasures. Such scheduling not only helps a child to remember what must be done but also to develop the idea that work comes before play.

A child will occasionally forget to follow through on assignments. You may also forget sometimes for days on end. The responsibilities should be revived when this happens, however, because they have been established and generally accepted by the family as part of the contribution made by the child.

If there are two or more children in a family who range in age from six to twelve, an interesting opportunity to foster responsibility and cooperation exists. If an eleven- or twelve-year-old is a responsible and mature youngster and the younger children are cooperative, parents can have the oldest child baby-sit if parents are nearby, not gone for long, and available by telephone. A parent can pay the oldest child about thirty-five cents per hour for sitting and the younger child can receive ten or fifteen cents per hour for being a good "sittee." The children should understand that *no one* will get paid if there is trouble that comes to the parents' attention. It is delightful to see children who might bicker three or four times per day cooperate with each other under these circumstances.

The suggestions for housework in Table 12 may be used as regular responsibilities for no pay or as additional sources of income for the child.

Table 12.   Ages Ten to Twelve

Job	Salary*
Clean outdoor furniture	$.50
Unload groceries (from car to house)	.05
Sweep sidewalk	.10
Wash outside of car	.75
Clean inside of car	.50
Give dog a bath	.25
Water lawn or plants (for ten minutes)	.10
Take out garbage (all garbage in house to the street)	.10
Feed dog	.05
Give dog water	.05
Brush dog (for fifteen minutes)	.10
Sweep porch	.10
Pull weeds (one large lawn bag)	.75
Rake leaves and pine needles	.50
Vacuum and sweep house	.75
Straighten up house (put away magazine, newspapers, belongings)	.25
Make bed	.05
Polish all of own shoes	.15
Walk dog	.15
Polish furniture	.50
Go to store	.50
Clean off dining room table	.10
Wash dishes	.30
Put away dishes (unload dishwasher)	.10
Clean closet (completely)	.30

*Average of $.40 per hour

Bedtimes

In most families, the ten-year-old should retire at approximately 9:00 P.M. on school nights and 10:00 P.M. on summer and weekend nights. The eleven-year-old should retire at about 9:00 P.M.

on school nights also but by approximately 10:30 P.M. on summer and weekend nights. The twelve-year-old should retire about 9:30 P.M. on school nights and before 11:00 P.M. on summer and weekend nights.

Some children retire early out of natural fatigue, and for these children bedtimes are not necessary. Bedtimes do provide a great deal of continuity and security for the child, however, and they also help parents maintain consistent limits.

Some children, especially with the advent of bussing to both public and private schools, must arise very early, and for these children an earlier bedtime might be necesary.

Other children may go to schools on split sessions and attend only in the afternoon. The recommended bedtimes should probably not be extended for these children. Rather, they should get up in the morning at a reasonable hour. This may be a good time for these children to do chores or to complete their homework. Rising early could be especially good for children who tend to have memory problems or learning disabilities.

Sometimes parents forget that children generally need a great deal more sleep than adults. It is difficult indeed for a fatigued child to perform well in school or have a happy disposition.

The "games" and other types of stalling tactics common among young children should have diminished by age ten. If not, then discipline in the home is probably on shaky ground. Parents should take a close look at setting up a disciplinary structure in conjunction with the responsibilities, bedtimes, and other aspects of discipline mentioned in this book.

If a child does continue to stall at bedtime, the amount of delay can be doubled and subtracted from his bedtime the next night. Thus, if a ten-year-old who should be in bed at 9:00 P.M. on a school night stalls until 9:15 P.M. the extra fifteen minutes is doubled to equal a half hour and subtracted from bedtime the next night so that the child must retire at 8:30 P.M.

Daylight Savings Time may present a problem because of the longer amount of daylight. The difference between a child's regular bedtime and darkness during Daylight Savings Time can be split down the middle. For example, if a child's bedtime is 8:30

P.M. and it is not dark until 9:00 P.M. bedtime should be 8:45 P.M.

It may take up to half an hour for a child of this age to fall asleep once in bed. The child should be allowed to read or generally relax for fifteen minutes or so before attempting to sleep if necessary. It is rather unusual for a child in this age range to need an hour to fall asleep more than once a week, to have a very restless sleep, or to awaken during the night.

If restlessness occurs on a regular basis, parents should take a look at the demands, expectations, and frustrations affecting the child. Problems may not be easily discernable at first, because sleep problems probably reflect the child's attempt to "forget" more basic problems that he or she may not be aware of. If an unusual sleep pattern extends several months, professional consultation with the pediatrician is indicated.

Allowance

The weekly allowance for ten-year-olds should be approximately sixty-five cents, for eleven-year-olds, ninety cents, and for twelve-year-olds, $1.20. Ten-year-olds should put ten cents into savings or contributions. The eleven-year-old should also put ten cents away for contributions or savings, and the twelve-year-old should commit fifteen cents per week.

If the child receives great "windfalls" in gifts from parents or relatives, this will result in an "inflationary economy." For that reason monetary gifts should be restricted to a maximum of one dollar during this age range and the balance should go into savings.

Spending

How should the child spend allowance? Allowance is provided so that a child can "squander" the money initially. Eventually the child will discover that trinkets and cheap articles will not hold up and should then be encouraged to save up to buy more expensive, better quality goods.

Allowance is not used, then, for school lunches, items of clothing, or any *necessity*. It is all used in the *luxury* area and it is the parent's obligation to provide for basic needs. On the other hand, when your child attends an occasional movie or other event, you should consider paying for this, and the child may use the allowance for refreshments. If the event the child wishes to attend is a luxury from the family's standpoint, then the child might save the allowance, with parents contributing 50 percent of the cost of attending.

Punishment

Physical punishment in this age range has lost most of its effectiveness, and it is generally not an acceptable way to discipline a child.

In terms of the three major approaches to deal with misbehavior —reflecting feelings, reasoning, and social restrictions—the first and third are still of primary importance, although reasoning is more important from age ten on. Parents must be careful not to be trapped into long reasoning discussions without either reflecting the child's feelings or following through with some type of social discipline.

Here again, if parents pretend that each word is worth $1, they should realize the poor exchange when the child spends $2 saying "I won't" and the parent, in return, spends $50 giving a lecture on the importance of responsibility.

One of the key principles here is to have discipline follow as soon as posible after negative behavior. Ideally, this would fall at least on the same day in which the negative behavior occurred. It is still important at this age level not to have long-term punishments for negative behavior—for example, restricting a child for six weeks because of poor grades or an infraction of rules. Parents should be wary about sending a child to his or her room as a punishment, especially if this room has many toys, games, books, and other desirable materials.

The real answer to disciplinary problems, as with emotional problems and behaviors that vary from the norm, is found in the positive relationship between the parents and the child. In addition, appropriate responsibilities set up by the family will provide the child with structure and avoid a great need for discipline.

Chapter 5 discusses responsibilities and structure in detail.

Physical Contact

Children in this age range have less interest in physical contact with their parents, but they usually still appreciate it and parents should not avoid an occasional touch on the arm, a pat on the back, and especially a good-night kiss. The child is now growing to old to be sitting on a parent's lap, however.

Sometimes parents, especially fathers, "play fight" with their children as a form of affection and interaction. But it is up to the parent to stop this type of activity before it proceeds to the point at which the child might hurt a parent or sibling, become emotionally upset with this activity, or see it as a competitive battle. If these types of activities are not enjoyed by both parent and child, they should certainly not be forced. If a child has some trouble falling asleep at night, then roughhousing before bedtime should be discouraged.

Self-Esteem

Girls may have more difficulty than boys maintaining self-esteem at this age because they have lost the cuteness of the little girl and are still not ready to socialize extensively. Generally, there are few activities or programs for girls during this age period, while boys have access to many activities, especially sports. A girl who has only average or below average grades and is not particularly attractive can feel this reduction of self-esteem significantly. We have found that this is frequently the case during this period of growth and awkwardness. Activities such as horseback riding, swimming, art, and music lessons may be ego-building areas for a girl, although competitive sports should not be discouraged if the girl has the capability to enjoy them and be proficient.

School

The ten-year-old with no learning or teacher problem likes school and teachers. He views them as a means of satisfying his love to learn. He works best in the structure of a time schedule and for teachers who are firm but fair and show that they like all students.

We occasionally find a ten-year-old who previously was eager to learn but has become more critical and demanding where school experiences are concerned. This often signals growing maturity and decisiveness. The teacher has become more important, and the child enjoys the teacher who tells funny stories or points out weaknesses in a light manner.

Children in this age group need to feel sure of the expectations people have of them, and as a result, they feel secure when given clear routine. The child is able to work on long-term assignments but needs to be checked periodically. Many parents observe that their children are not able to cope with the "middle school" at this age. The number of moves and the lack of structure during the day can be overwhelming.

Within school the basic emphasis for the ten-, eleven-, and twelve-year-old is on learning to read in areas such as science, social studies, and mathematics. We have found that the reading level of social studies and science textbooks are usually from one to three years above the grade level in which they are used. If a child has a deficit in reading, consider reading to him from a textbook and let the child answer questions on his own. Such a child might require special assistance at this point.

Some children at this age may still reverse letters such as "b" and "d" when writing, or reverse words such as "was" and "saw" when reading. These difficulties are an indication that perhaps the child has difficulty in perceiving left and right or cannot project directions from his body out into space. The parent is referred to Chapter 7 for procedures that will aid the development of "directionality."

Chapter 7 may also help parents with children experiencing the following reading difficulties: recognition of a word in one part of a paragraph but not in another part, inability to develop a sight vocabulary, and inability to correlate letters or combinations of letters with the sounds they represent. The examples given in Chapter 7 are to be used with a younger child and ten- through twleve-year-olds should be able to perform at a more sophisticated level.

If a child has difficulty reading textbooks, parents may wish to secure cassette tape recording copies of these textbooks from the

Institute for the Blind in Washington, D.C. Many are recorded and are on file at the institute. The child then can read the textbook and hear it being read at the same time.

If a child has writing problems, parents may wish to contact the school and make arrangements for oral examinations to be given in any test that requires lengthy answers. If a child is having trouble remembering what a teacher is saying in class, parents may wish to make arrangements for the child to use a tape recorder during lecture courses. The child with writing or memory problems can be aided by the exercises suggested in Chapter 7.

Some children are highly distractible and may find it necesssary to work in a study carrel to concentrate more effectively. The distractible child definitely should be placed in a self-contained classroom and not in a pod or open-space classroom. This child should also do homework in a quiet, nondistracting place in the house.

By this age children should have developed easily flowing cursive handwriting. However, some children still display underdeveloped eye-hand coordination or may develop very cramped writing. If eye-hand coordination is a difficulty for a child, parents should refer to Chapter 6 and engage the child in the eye-hand exercises outlined there.

A child may still have difficulty performing the relaxed rhythmic patterns of writing even if eye-hand coordination is adequate. A child's fingers might become pinched and cramped, and it will be difficult for the child's hand to move across the page while writing. One procedure that might help here is to take a cork float, like the ones used in fishing, bore a hole through its center, and insert a pencil into the hole. The child should grasp the pencil so that the cork is in the palm of the hand. This will help him to remain relaxed. A mechanical aid that can be purchased from Zaner-Bloser Company, 612 North Park Street, Columbus, Ohio 43215, is the Writing Frame together with the Finger Fitting Primary Pencil. Together, the frame and pencil can aid in correcting hand position and arm movement. Samples of writing exercises that will help a child develop a good rhythmic flow in writing are given in Figure 6.

Although some children have beautifully formed letters, writ-

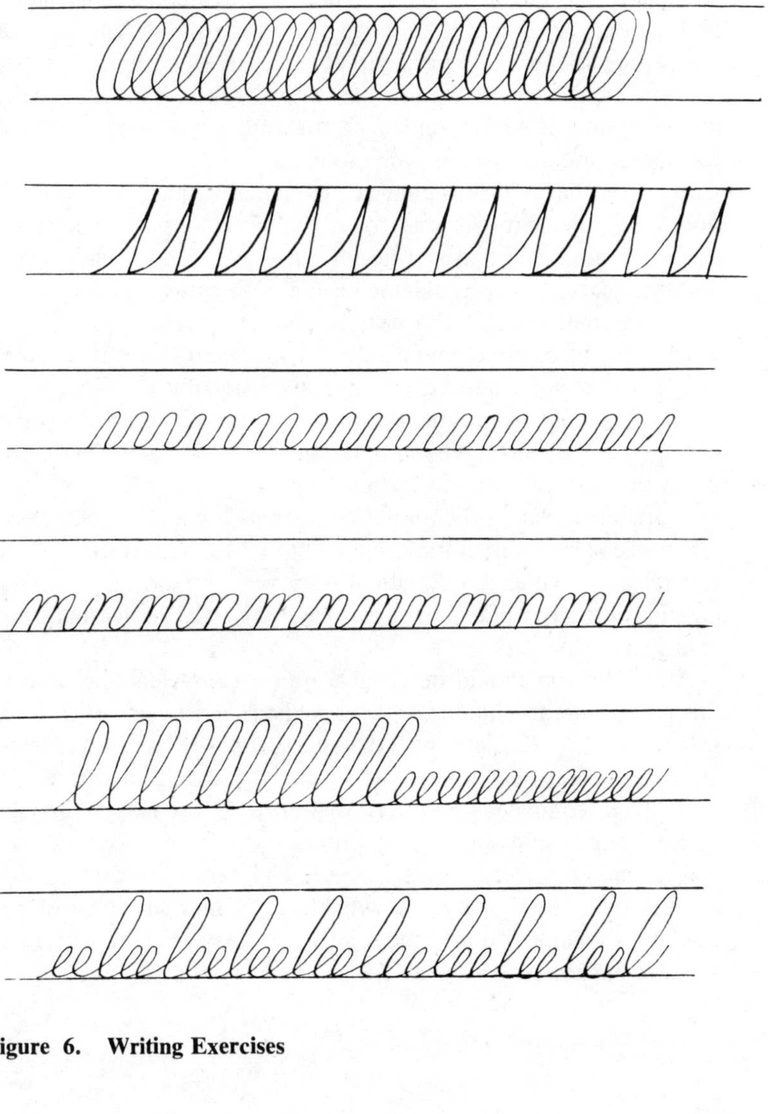

Figure 6. Writing Exercises

ing might be a tedious task. This can result in poor grades because daily assignments might be performed too slowly or not completed. If the quantity of written work is the problem, it will be helpful to have daily sessions in which sentences are written from dictation or a written paragraph is given to the child to copy while he or she is timed. This same paragraph can be repeated day after day with the child trying to reduce the length of time it takes to write the paragraph. If writing remains a frustrating task, parents should consider a course in typing for the child.

We often hear that a youngster is unable to master long division. This frequently is due to an inability to put numbers in proper columns. The use of graph paper will help a child learn both the placement of problems on the page as well as the placement of numbers into the proper columns.

Perhaps the most common difficulty in long division is inability to cope with the sequence of steps. Occasionally a child cannot remember which step follows which. A simple reference chart stating: (A) divide, (B) multiply, (C) subtract, and (D) bring down the next number, will often help.

If after completing the above suggestions for a child with these school academic difficulties the child is still described by the teacher as "daydreaming, inattentive, reversing words and letters, not finishing his work, having poor writing, etc.," a learning disability might be present.

An evaluation should be sought from a competent resource at this point. Parents should consult a pediatrician to find such a resource. It is not too late. In the authors' experience, ten-, eleven-, and twelve-year-old children who have a learning disability can profit from competent remedial assistance. If a child of this age desires help, rapid and major progress can occur. But do not delay. Once the teenage years arrive, children with learning disabilities will often give up in school. They find social participation and widening interests more attractive than sticking with tedious and unsuccessful schoolwork.

9 The Early Teen Years

The thirteen- to fifteen-year-old presents the most difficult period in terms of "getting obstacles off of the track." Actually, children in the period between thirteen and fifteen face many obstacles—both real and imaginary.

A commonly held but erroneous belief about this age group is that it is when children enter the so-called youth culture or when a "generation gap" begins to form. Only a small percentage of children in this age range believe that there is a generation gap separating them from their parents. Parents should not succumb to the information presented by the media, the alarm tactics of many "crisis-seekers," and the fostering of these concepts by certain teen magazines or movies that hope to tap this wealthy market. The media often report the statements and actions of a small minority of this age group because they make for exciting viewing and reading. The crisis-seeker, whose function and interest is presented in Chapter 2, is concerned with only a minority, and the magazines, movies or other businesses that earn their incomes from the youth culture are often reprehensible and to be scorned.

Some of the more realistic obstacles a thirteen- to fifteen-year-old child faces are "family-splitters," democratic child-rearing, changing community factors, and physical and chemical changes within the child.

The family-splitters have been discussed fully in Chapter 2 and are many: consolidated schools, television, the working mother, too much involvement by parents in business and community affairs. They can all serve to dilute the family's effectiveness and reduce parent-child contact.

The democratic or laissez-faire family, in which children have equal decision-making authority, can bring confusion and insecurity to the child. While the child at this age needs greater participation with the family in terms of expressing ideas, opinions, and participating in the decision-making process, parents must continue to maintain the final authority for major family decisions and those concerned with values.

If parents believe their children are able to take care of themselves at this point because of their growing maturity, or because parents believe they do not understand the youth culture, the child may see this as neglect and can certainly fall under the influence of a negative peer group. This *can* lead to drug problems and a lessening of moral values.

Children want to participate in family affairs and want to have a say in the decision-making process, but they respect their parents' judgment and authority. On the other hand, some parents do not respect their children as individuals and do not understand their feelings and thoughts. They can also drive their children into groups of similarly rejected or neglected youth who are in trouble and will influence their associates adversely.

Changes in the community during the past two decades have had a profound influence on the child of this age. Today many young teenagers lack a feeling of being part of a neighborhood, and they are unable to participate with peers because they aren't old enough to drive. Residential and commercial areas have been separated in larger communities. Thus, the child does not get to know the community and is often isolated from contact with adults.

Children at this age are undergoing many chemical, physical, and emotional changes at a rapid rate. They will often be different from their peers in some aspect of development. Children do not tolerate differences in each other at this stage because they are insecure themselves. They are highly critical of one another and have a strong need to conform.

What can we as parents do to help remove these various obstacles from our children's paths? We cannot simply adopt the values and community standards that were prevalent a generation ago.

If parents can reject the mystery of the so-called youth culture, they will have taken a step in the right direction. The average adolescent shares a majority of values with parents. These include positive views toward hard work, competition, the need for structure and authority, and a respect for private property, individual effort, and autonomy. Most youth have pride in and concern for their community and a great deal of affection and loyalty for their families. If parents can recognize these facts and have more confidence in their own judgment and ability to lead their children, they will go a long way toward correcting problems frequently seen in children of this age.

Parents can include their children in family discussions concerning family finances, work responsibilities, community commitments, and make straightforward statements regarding their personal values. Parents must be very aware of a child's feelings and give ample opportunity for free discussion and exchange of ideas, while maintaining family structure and authority.

It is important that parents develop friendships with other dedicated parents and expose their children to these friends and their families. In this way, the children are able to see their parents interact with other adults, and they might use these other parents as resources on occasions when they might feel more free to talk with someone other than their own parents. Children are sometimes better able to discuss problems with people outside the family, and this type of arrangement ensures that these people will share many of the same values as the family. By associating closely with other families in this way, parents will be able, in effect, to develop their own subculture, which can give experience and strength to the child.

Schools must also continue to provide structure, security, and positive models for children to emulate in addition to a strong basic academic emphasis. The large, unwieldy, consolidated junior high school or "little high school" (and, in our view, the newer "middle school") has not been successful in this regard. Schools can make studies more relevant by teaching children about their own communities, their traditions and values and their leaders, who can serve as models. Excellence in achievement, behavior, and creativity should be rewarded in concrete terms with special awards and privileges.

Certain types of teacher-led group discussions can be valuable. Children can grow positively through group discussions, if these discussions are not reserved for or centered on the children who are creating problems. The group leaders should not focus on criticism of the family, the school, institutions, or the community as we have often seen. School leaders support positive aspects of the community and must protect their students from ridiculing each other at school much as the parent must handle sibling rivalry and scapegoating within the family.

Responsibilities

Thirteen- through fifteen-year-olds should be expected to perform three responsibilities per day and an additional one hour of work time per week. Pay the thirteen-year-old seventy-five cents per hour, the fourteen-year-old, eighty cents per hour, and the fifteen-year-old, eighty-five cents per hour.

Work is much more important at this age both as a source of self-esteem for the child and as a provider of money, which is growing in importance. Children of this age may begin to work outside the home cutting lawns for neighbors or even in some cases be regularly employed, although special work permits may be needed for a child younger than sixteen.

It is unfortunate that fourteen- and fifteen-year-old children who are capable and eager to work do not have the legal opportunity to do so. Because of baby-sitting opportunities, girls at this age are fortunate. Many of the problems of this age group are produced by boredom and a lack of meaningful activities. It is striking to see children at this age who have difficulties in school and who are not talented athletically do well in a job and be described by their employers as hardworking and conscientious.

If a child is spending long hours working and spending up to two hours in study time per day, parents may wish to cut down on the regular responsibilities and work time required in the home. Sometimes parents feel they should not pay an allowance when their child is working and earning an income, but the child needs the steady allowance because it symbolizes parental care and interest. A small number of selected responsibilities need not be very time consuming, and the young person who is working can still have time to carry out at least one or two daily responsibilities. If a child is overexerting, we usually find this due to an excessive number of activities or the presence of learning problems that require an inordinate amount of time for homework.

The suggestions for housework in Table 13 may be used as regular responsibilities without pay or as additional sources of income for the child.

Chapter 5 discusses a procedure that can be used with a young teen to add external control and additional motivation for accomplishment of specific skills, chores, or tasks.

Curfew/Dating

A thirteen- and fourteen-year-old should not attend a social event alone or with peers unless there is adequate supervision by adults or older brothers or sisters. This is not to say that a child at this age cannot congregate in a neighborhood area in daylight hours. Somewhat more latitude should be given to the fifteen-year-old, but remember: even if a fifteen-year-old looks like an adult, he or she is not mature in terms of judgment and self-control. Parents are referred to the chart in Chapter 2 that deals with evening time limits.

A few parents allow their twelve- and thirteen-year-old daughters to date on an individual basis without supervision and without a designated place or activity. This is asking for trouble. Sometimes parents are overly impressed by the apparent maturity of their rapidly developing daughters. Some parents push young children into maturity by encouraging the application of makeup and the wearing of revealing attire.

The rapidly maturing girl does have some special difficulties and may feel out of place at times among her giggling and physi-

Table 13.   Ages Thirteen through Fifteen

Job	Salary*
Shovel snow	$1.00
Wash car (outside)	1.50
Wax car	2.00
Clean car (inside)	.50
Clean garage or basement (sweeping, hosing, throw away junk)	.75
Give dog a bath	.30
Take out garbage (from all areas of house to street)	.15
Brush dog (for fifteen minutes)	.25
Pull weeds (one large lawn bag)	1.00
Fertilize lawn	1.50
Mow lawn	2.00
Trim grass along sidewalks	1.00
Trim hedges	1.50
Rake leaves and pine needles	1.00
Vacuum and sweep house	1.00
Clean bathroom floors	.75 each
Clean kitchen floor	.50
Clean windows and sliding glass doors	.20 each
Wash screens	.25 each
Polish silver	1.00
Polish furniture	.75
Paint	.85 per hour
Go to store and do shopping	1.00
Babysit younger children	.50 per hour
Wash dishes and/or load dishwasher	.50

*Average $.85 per hour

cally immature classmates. Parents must remember that this four-teen- or fifteen-year-old is still basically a child. While parents must never ridicule their daughter's development, they must recognize that she is still a child despite her protestations.

The thirteen-year-old should be able to participate in mixed social functions under the supervision of responsible school personnel and responsible parents. Some fourteen-year-olds seem capable of "dating" in group situations where supervision is available and reliable. Some fifteen-year-old girls can be trusted to date sixteen- or seventeen-year-old boys on an individual basis once or twice a month. However, this event should have clearly specified limits in terms of time and acceptable activity. The full privileges of individual dating involving relatively unspecified events ("going to the movies") should be postponed to age sixteen.

Parents should not succumb to arguments such as "Everybody that I know does that" or "If I wanted to get in trouble, I could do it." The purpose of requiring structure and limits is not because of a lack of parental trust in a child but to protect the child from uncomfortable situations and to give him or her a way to escape peer pressure.

Sex

Children at this age should be given information covering a wide area of sex-related topics. This includes not only information about the biology of sex as covered in the nine to twelve year age range, but also the psychology, customs, and attitudes relating to sex and the various problems surrounding sex such as prostitution and venereal disease.

Any discussion of sex should be tied in with the *values* that the parent hopes to teach. Sexual behavior cannot be handled in a vacuum, and it is part and parcel of the individual's values. This is one of the problems of sex education in the public schools. Most public schools believe that they are not allowed to teach religious and moral values in sex education. Therefore, the *"value"* that sexual behavior and values are not related to one another is inadvertently often taught instead.

Parents should not feel badly if they are embarrassed to discuss this very personal area or if they have difficulty answering questions regarding their own value systems as they apply to sexual behavior. Much of this can be covered through books and other reading materials in the library. Be careful, however. Many of the books in the public library may not endorse the value system of a particular family. *Young People and Sex* by Arthur Cain is recommended.

Sexual intercourse at the thirteen to fifteen year old range is very unusual, especially full sexual relations on a regular basis. This is true despite frequent reports to the contrary by the media.

The child of this age who participates in sexual intercourse is certainly not liberated but is typically lost and perhaps responding to peer pressure.

If this is occurring with a child, parents must be firm and tell the child to stop participating sexually. This request should be made on the basis of the family moral values, the child's reputation, and the very real problems of pregnancy and disease. In terms of stressing loss of reputation, we have seen children curtail sexual activity when realizing that friends can be lost. The child needs to learn that his or her friends, or the majority of peers that the child respects, will not see this activity as daring after a short period of time, but rather consider the child to have a problem.

Girls who wear extremely short skirts, see-through blouses, or other provocative types of clothing in this thirteen to fifteen range are also asking for trouble. They should be prohibited from this type of dress by their parents. No lengthy explanations are necessary. Lack of respect by peers can be brought up as a primary reason. Appearing seductive can prevent the child from getting to know others and prevent long lasting relationships.

Smoking

Smoking in the thirteen to fifteen age group should be prohibited. Parents can point out the usual reasons—but stress health. If parents suspect that smoking is taking place, it should be prohibited in the home with the hope that the child will give it up away from home. It is not a good idea to build the area of smoking into a "spy game" with great conflict between parent and child.

Bedtime

The thirteen-year-old should retire to his or her room at approximately 10:00 P.M. on school nights, 11:30 on summer nights, and midnight on weekend nights. The fourteen-year-old and fifteen-year-old should be in bed about 10:30 P.M. on school nights and be self-regulated on summer and weekend nights. A bedtime should never interfere with the entire family's evening pattern. For example, if a fourteen-year-old decides to stay up until 1:00 A.M. on a weekend night watching television, the television should not be so loud that it interferes with other people's sleep. This child should also be able to get up the next morning on time so that a bedtime does not interfere with normally scheduled routine.

The thirteen- to fifteen-year-old may have more special week-night events because of school functions, sports activities, or other activities that require later bedtimes. Parents should be careful about extending the school night bedtime, however, because the child must learn that work takes precedence over play.

T.V./Movies

A thirteen- to fifteen-year-old child should be able to watch unlimited television except for old R-rated movies that occasionally appear on television at almost any time of the day or night. In addition, there are some sophisticated talk shows and comedies that should be avoided. These shows, in which family values and community institutions are constantly questioned or ridiculed, and where the slick and superficial individual is highly valued, can be dangerous. But even some of these shows may be acceptable if parents watch with the child and both child and parents discuss a show's pros and cons and its values.

R-rated movies are out for children of this age. Parents must be aware that sometimes older siblings will take their younger brothers and sisters to R-rated movies, thinking that they are being helpful in liberating their younger siblings. This should not be allowed. Many of these movies are poor learning experiences for a child. They often contain questionable sexual morality and stress anti-family, anti-establishment, and violent themes. They tend to make heroes out of drug users, motorcycle gangs, and other misfits.

Allowance

The weekly allowance for a thirteen-year-old should be $1.65 with twenty-five cents to be withheld by the child for savings or contributions to church or charities. The fourteen-year-old receives an allowance of $2.25 with thirty cents withheld for charitable contributions and savings, and the fifteen-year-old receives a $2.75 allowance with thirty-five cents withheld for savings and contributions. The child in this age range has a larger allowance but may have legitimate ways of spending it because of broadened social contacts. Parents may choose to contribute to some luxury entertainment, such as movies, even though the child may have sufficient cash from time to time to take care of this. The child of this age should not be allowed to keep more than $3 or $4 of a gift. The rest should go to savings.

Because, as mentioned earlier, actual employment is usually not available, parents may wish to find legitimate work around the home so that a child can earn additional income. The teenager should be given some of the more interesting and responsible chores in the home, not just the menial ones.

Clothing

If the purchase of clothing, which is ordinarily paid for by the parents, becomes a point of contention and family bickering, parents might consider a quarterly clothing budget for the child. Parents should indicate the type and general style of clothing to be purchased, and the child should select the specific items.

Fears/Shyness

Most specific, consistent, and irrational fears have dropped out by this age but may remain to a very mild degree. If a child would prefer to sleep with a night light because of a mild uneasiness with the dark, for example, no issue should be made. There may be an increased shyness around members of the opposite sex, and often children of this age are beginning to prefer not being seen with their parents in public. These feelings will decrease in time and should be ignored.

Many times fear is precipitated by a change in schools, which forces a child to enter a new social group whose groupings and cliques have already been formed. In this situation, the shyness is a result of real conditions, but with time the child should become accepted. In this case, the child should attempt to make one or two friends rather than trying to be generally popular, and the parents can help by allowing or encouraging their child to invite a friend over to watch television or spend the night.

Shy children of this age might be encouraged to answer the telephone at home, to greet each person they see during the day, and engage in other activities that will provide social experience. Often shy children are participating in a vicious circle: they are not good listeners because they are attempting to think about what to say next and not listening.

Everyone likes a good listener and children must be helped to see that if they relax, listen well, and ask questions about what interests other people, they can become more popular. It is often helpful for a child to participate in activities in school that foster communications, even if only in indirect ways. For example, working as part of a stage crew for the drama club can give a child the opportunity to "rub elbows" with others. Recurring and intense fears should receive professional consultation.

Anger and Tears

Explosive anger and a teary and whining disposition may develop as a result of adolescent changes. Thirteen- and fourteen-year-old girls often seem to lose their psychological balance for a period of a year or so because of chemical and physical changes taking place within them. Parents must be careful not to respond to these outbursts by overreacting or reacting in a way similar to the child.

Spanking is rarely a good way to deal with these outbursts and should seldom if ever be used during this period. Parents need to ride out this temporary storm, provide much positive support, and maintain limits.

The early adolescent may appear more fatigued, require greater amounts of sleep, and generally tend to be grouchier than previously. Sometimes parents will be able to notice that the remarks and whining complaints made by the teenager are not representative of what the child is really thinking. The child may also appear puzzled at the crankiness. Lengthy reasoning can be helpful at this time if parents can avoid being manipulated by the child.

In spite of the frequent presence of these characteristics, there is no reason for a child of this age to be destructive or harmful. The child who has daily temper outbursts, fights at school or in the neighborhood, maliciously destroys property, or sets fires should receive professional consultation.

Parent Control

Occasionally a mother will state that she can no longer control her fourteen- or fifteen-year-old son because he is too large and strong. If she has been basing her control on physical strength up to this time, she has been proceeding in a foolish manner. Control over children should be based primarily upon a positive relationship developed through shared experiences. If a child disobeys, a mother can bring the father into the situation when he returns from work. If there is no father in the family, then an uncle, family friend, or other person may have to become involved.

Parents have many other types of controls and leverages, however, such as meals, allowances, and other factors that are usually taken for granted by the child. An off-the-record visit by a juvenile authority or police officer may be helpful in a preventive sense if the situation is sufficiently out of control to warrant such a move. Repeated aggressiveness, outbursts, or rebelliousness may reflect emotional, neurological, or drug-related problems.

Cry for Help

Sometimes girls will write letters to friends that describe explicit sexual experiences, plans to be truant from school or to run away from home. Usually these accounts represent fantasy and are a means to gain attention and popularity from an undesirable friend or peer group. Frequently, it represents a cry for help to the family. These letters may represent the child's need for more positive interaction with parents or more structure or limits.

Parents should not be concerned about intrusion into a child's privacy when letters of this type are left about the house. Parents of the other child should be called and if there is no cooperation on the matter, then the children's association should be broken off. This type of action can also signal emotional difficulties and the need for professional consultation.

Running Away

Running away may also represent a cry for help and the child may be truly unhappy regarding circumstances within the home, school, or community. Unhappiness will almost always have shown up prior to the child's having run away and be found in areas of behavior or deviation from the norm in terms of inhibition, fearfulness, aggression, sleep problems, and behavior problems.

Running away is sometimes a simple "lark" in which the child is influenced by peers and merely wants to experience the excitement of leaving home overnight. In almost all cases of running away, even when the child is seriously upset over something, he or she can usually be found close to home or at a friend's house. If the child actually does leave the city and does not try to notify parents directly or indirectly, this indicates a much more serious problem.

Sometimes adolescents are aware that after they run away from home and return they are rewarded by luxuries and extra privileges because of parental fear and guilt. If this occurs, frequently more attempts at "blackmail" will occur.

If a child runs away from home and the parents do not know where he or she is through tips from friends or their parents and if the child is not home by midnight, the police should be asked to bring the child home. If the child has contacted his parents and is with a friend and in good circumstances, it is often wise for the parents to let the child know they are aware of the child's whereabouts and to allow the child to remain away for several days to permit the conflict to "cool."

When the child returns, the main focus of discussion should center on areas of unhappiness in the community, home, or peer group. Often parents do not know what to tell their children or whether they should discipline them for running away. Emotions frequently run high at these times. Discussions regarding punishment need not take place as soon as the child returns home, and parents can tell their children quite frankly that they plan some disciplinary measure but want to think about it for a day or two.

Usually, grounding the child for three weeks with deprivation of television rights and other privileges will be sufficient. This punishment will not prevent the child from running away again. But it must take place to handle cases of manipulation as well as providing consistency in terms of family discipline and structure. Parents should not forget the effect it may have on siblings also. Spoiled and manipulative children who are repeatedly responding to peer pressure may sometimes benefit from "jail therapy." One or two nights in a juvenile detention center can sometimes be very constructive, but parents should never allow placement in a city of county jail.

Drugs

This is a period when children may experiment with marijuana, alcohol, or other drugs. It is often difficult to tell when a child is using drugs, but if he or she become reclusive, appears glassy-eyed, slurs speech, and associates with known drug users, parents should be greatly concerned.

Children using marijuana over a period of time will usually have changes in their behavior, becoming unambitious, irritable, and passive. Grades and school activities will usually suffer greatly. The child is usually not aware of these changes and develops a set of rationalizations to explain behavior and defend usage of drugs. A child who has not lied frequently in the past may lie constantly to protect usage, friends, and the source of the drug supply.

While a child's privacy should be protected at any age, it is imperative for the parent to search a child's room and belongings when drug usage is suspected. If drug abuse is caught early, protecting and isolating the child from the drug peer group, renewed family interactions, and professional counseling can prevent a recurrence. If the child denies continued drug use but still associates with the same peer group and deterioration in behavior and school performance continues, parents should assume that the child is using drugs and take more drastic steps. Programs that embody intensive positive peer pressure and isolation from the old peer group appear to offer the most hope for success at this time.

Once a child has developed a dependency on drugs and a commitment to the drug culture, parental discussions, various forms of discipline, and even professional counseling can be futile. Sometimes parents believe they can stop the drug usage by curtailing all monies given to the child, but these drugs are readily available. Sometimes a lack of money may encourage a child to begin selling drugs.

Sibling Rivalry

Sibling rivalry can be handled by discussions, by separating the children for a short period of time, or by other methods of discipline. The child at this age can often be approached through reasoning and counseled not to let a younger brother or sister cause them to lose their "cool." An appeal to the child's maturity, extra privileges, and extended social contacts can often help a child to feel less threatened by younger siblings.

Because a child needs a great deal of privacy at this age, younger siblings should not be allowed to meddle in the older child's affairs, whether this has to do with possessions or with friends.

One situation appears guaranteed to produce quibbling siblings: the long automobile trip. Fortunately, in an automobile it is easier to determine who starts a particular disagreement, and rules can be set down so that a child will lose a privilege when the family arrives at its destination. For example, loss of one-half hour swimming time for each violation or loss of television time. It is important to understand that arguments in a car are common. Parents should not generalize from this situation and believe that the children do not like each other or that they do not have control over their children.

Divorce

If there is a divorce, a child should be spared the "gruesome details." Divorce is covered more thoroughly in Chapter 7. Just because a child has reached adolescence, he or she is not prepared to hear sordid details regarding either of the parent's problems.

Parents must be cautious about decisions regarding custody of the child when a divorce occurs. Some parents and attorneys feel that a child at this age should be prepared to determine which family, community, and school environment is best for him or her. This can cause great problems for the child in terms of loyalties and self-concept. If at all possible, decisions regarding custody should be made by the parents or the court. If the child has definite and strong feelings in one direction, this can certainly be incorporated into the decision, which must ultimately be made by adults.

Shoplifting

The incidence of shoplifting has increased rapidly in recent years, and there is considerable peer pressure among teenagers for this behavior. While shoplifting may represent only responding to a dare or seeking to please a peer group, parental response should be swift and firm. Items should be immediately returned to the store owner or manager, or monetary restitution should be made by the child. Additional discipline should be administered such as extra work at home or removal of privileges.

The child who shoplifts repeatedly and without peer influence may be asking for help from the parents in terms of positive interaction or greater attention and structure.

Death

Upon the death of a member of the family or a close relative, a youngster should participate in all of the rituals of the funeral. As with younger children, parents should not attempt to protect the child from their grief but rather share this grief as a family so that all may experience the emotional loss. If the child does not cry or show grief, it may affect the child in unfortunate ways in the future. If a parent is certain that a child has not grieved—publicly or when alone—a private discussion about the tragedy with one or more trusted adults might help elicit a proper emotional response.

Tenderness

Children of this age range may pull back somewhat from physical contact with parents and may not wish to be seen with parents when certain members of their peer group are present. Parents should not feel alarmed or threatened by this turn of events and should respect the child's wishes. Parents should not pull back themselves however, but should continue to touch and show physical attention at home. Don't be surprised if a child pulls back as though he or she has been touched by an electric current. If the child tells his parents that they are too "mushy" or in other ways indicates an aversion to being touched, parents may have to back off for a period of time while the child grows out of this stage.

Intellectual Slowness

Children who have below average intellectual ability may be unmotivated in school. They could be overwhelmed by a full day of academic work and may benefit from a work-study program. In such a program they are able to participate in employment for a salary and spend only a few hours per day in school taking basic subjects. The school counselor can help set up a program of this type.

Many vocational programs are available in evening schools and vocational institutes for a child older than fifteen. In many cases, a state department of vocational rehabilitation or similar governmental agency is able to provide career counseling and vocational placement for children sixteen and older.

School

By age thirteen, children should be well along the road toward good study habits and independent work. They should not require more than occasional help with homework and should be able to set up their own study routines.

Thirteen-year-olds tend to be happier in school than eleven- or twelve-year-olds. They have a more organized approach to learning. They may refer to school rules as "stupid," but they like the structure rules offer since they really want freedom from making decisions.

For fourteen-year-olds, classwork may be tedious and "unnecessary." The ninth grader is frequently social minded and can become more involved with peers than classroom work.

Fifteen-year-olds learn quickly in new fields because they want to have many opinions and sufficient information to discuss them. They may find it easier to express themselves in an informal panel discussion or a "bull session," than in writing, which requires more "work."

If a child is having trouble with studying despite adequate intelligence and lack of learning disabilities, a regular study time should be set up and required to earn privileges each evening. This does not mean a child should simply spend a certain amount of time in a room. Parents should learn what the child is capable of doing during a given period of time and should superficially check the child's work each morning or other convenient time. Do this to determine if the child has earned privileges for that evening.

Many children have trouble concentrating at this age and they attempt to cover too much during a study period. Such a child should be encouraged to study for approximately twenty minutes and then take a five-minute break. This should be gradually extended to thirty minutes of study with a five-minute break.

The child should always study in the same place and away from distractions such as music or television. Sometimes it helps to actually contract with the child for grades expected with gradual improvement expected each grade period. No child should be expected to move from a C average across all subjects to a B average in one six-week period. This type of improvement might require as much as a year of school.

Children who have had corrective remediation for a learning disability may still have some residual problems. Children who still show weaknesses in auditory receptive areas should postpone foreign languages. If handwriting is still laborious and time consuming, the child might benefit from becoming proficient in typing.

Thirteen- to fifteen-year-old children are often striving for independence from family. If they are having difficulty with a certain subject in school or a particular teacher or feel they are being treated unfairly, they will resent parents making contact with the school. This resentment frequently is due to pressure from a child's peer group. The child might be afraid that the group will ridicule or ostracize him.

Parents should talk over school problems with their children. If children object to parental involvement, they should be assured that parents realize the children are older, and unless the issue involves a dangerous situation, the children should have an opportunity to work out the problem on their own. However, the parent should set a time limit for a child to complete such a task. It should be made clear that parents will make an effort to resolve the situation if the child has not worked out the problem by the agreed upon time.

When speaking to a teacher about a problem, parents may hear comments such as the child never has paper or pencil, skips class, or doesn't turn in homework. These are sometimes signs of a more basic problem, and punishment is usually not the answer.

A statement about not having paper and pencil might be made by a teacher in a class where many notes are required. The child may have poor or underdeveloped fine motor speed. To avoid frustration or embarrassment, the child might be appearing in class without paper and pencil.

The child may skip a class or arrive unprepared when an assignment is due that the child cannot complete because of weak academic skills. The child may also know he or she will be expected to read in front of the class and may not want to because of poor reading skills.

Some children may skip a day on which there is a test if they are academically deficient. Occasionally, children are aware that they are not prepared for a test because of difficulties they have in reading and understanding the material.

On the other hand, the child who skips school or arrives unprepared may be experiencing difficulties organizing material or placing it on paper. This type of child will perform more successfully on true-false or multiple-choice tests than on essay tests. Occasionally, professional intervention can result in obtaining an alternate mode of testing that is more suitable to a particular child.

The child who is described by a teacher as never turning in homework may be the most handicapped, educationally speaking. Here we may be talking about a student who has poor auditory or visual perception skills. This boy or girl may be unable to remember assignments given verbally. For example, the child might be trying to understand the first statement while the second and third are being given and thus become confused.

The child with poor auditory skills should not attempt a foreign language. Many foreign words differ only in the sound and spelling of their endings. The child with weak auditory discrimination or memory will have difficulty learning and remembering these words.

There is also the child whose parents have been told he or she is bright but is failing. This lack of motivation may be due to the lack of challenge in school, but it is more likely related to a learning disability. If the parents feel the child might have a learning disability, an evaluation should be sought from a competent source. The parents should consult with a pediatrician to find such a source.

By the time a child reaches mid to late teens, remediation of learning disabilities is much more formidable. Though positive results are certainly obtainable—even at this "late age"—the job is clearly more complex. With time fast running out, now is possibly the final feasible opportunity for parents to obtain professional help for their children.

10 The Mid to Late
Teen Years

Would you believe that many parents are frightened of their sixteen-, seventeen-, and eighteen-year-old children? Frightened and bewildered by them. This observation is curious in light of the fact that sixteen, seventeen, and eighteen year old youngsters are themselves frightened and bewildered by their world. Major factions within our society have produced a situation in which children have been forced to attempt to grow up too rapidly. Yet youngsters in this age range continue to be children in many respects.

Present laws state that the eighteen-year-old is an adult with full legal and moral responsibilities. Such laws can be, in many situations, very unfair to children and parents. Young adults or children of eighteen years of age cannot handle what someone twenty-one or thirty-one or forty-one years old can handle, yet they are charged with equal legal responsibility. Parents are told by many mental health professionals, school authorities, and often by the children themselves that they are no longer responsible for their offspring who are eighteen. Too frequently a split occurs between the child and the parents, which is prompted by forces totally beyond the control of the family.

Issues related to society's demands and obligations, vocational choices, college, dating, dependence, independence, financial demands, peer demands, and family demands, all become prominent and at times difficult issues during this age period. Parents can help to ease the discomfort by remembering that in spite of physical size, appearance, and occasionally the ideas and opinions expressed, most sixteen- to eighteen-year-olds need their parents—their guidance, their presence, their advice, and often their restrictions.

Although a person in this age range may occasionally behave in ways easily rejected by parents, the parents should attempt to continue guidance, both subtle and obvious. They should not reject or neglect the young adult, but rather continue to respect the child in spite of what may often appear to be irreconcilable or destructive circumstances.

Clothing

Adults should not attempt to join youth in this age range in their many activities, language, or style of dress. Young adults thirty years ago would rarely have considered purchasing a pair of blue suede shoes, pegged pants, or a "zoot suit." In reflecting on the state of affairs at that time, while parents generally did not *approve* of the dress of youth, they continued to give guidance and advice concerning dress, and they permitted their offspring, often with resigned chagrin, to dress in what the parents considered to be an outlandish fashion.

If it is true that some element of rebellion is necessary during this age period (perhaps independence from parents would be a better description) and the child seeks to convey this by dressing in the "uniform" of his peers, parents dressing in a fashion similar to their children could cause the young adult to become increasingly outlandish in asserting independence and differentness. It has been the authors' observation that on occasion teenage dress is both a manifestation of a child's desire to be like other youth and of the child's desire to be different from adults. If the parents do not permit the child to be different from them, the child is occasionally driven to more deviant clothing or rebellious behavior. Of course, proper dress for church, synagogue, school, dining out, and other similar occasions should reflect the values and "uniform" of the family.

Parents should make efforts to have children in this age range, particularly girls, dress in moderate and nonsexually disclosing fashion. In spite of the youngster's possible claims to the contrary, there are many youth who continue to dress in nonprovocative ways, and conservative dress simply makes life for the child in this age range less complicated.

Bedtimes/Home Times

It is commonly believed that the young person at this age should have no prescribed bedtimes because it may be demeaning. Often a person of this age will protest that peers have no regulated bedtimes. Although it may be true that the bedtime at this age does not serve an educational function, it is true that the young person is still a part of the family and should continue to fit into the cohesive family pattern. The child should not interfere with the rights and opportunities of other members of the family. If it makes no difference to the family when a child of this age retires and if there are no great problems in terms of discipline or relationships, then certainly both boys and girls might be permitted to regulate their bedtimes. If parents are apprehensive about bedtime for a youngster of this age, a general rule of thumb might pertain here: The child is not to be out of the home more than one hour beyond the parent's bedtime (unless the parent retires unusually early such as at 9 or 10 P.M.). Other appropriate regulations can be implemented by a parent concerned about proper bed/home times.

The sixteen-year-old should be able to participate two nights out per week with similar age friends until 9:30 P.M. and two nights per week until 11:00. In supervised group situations, of course, this time could be extended, just as for the fifteen-year-old.

The seventeen-year-old should be able to stay out most nights until 10:30 and two nights until 12:30. However, when a child goes out of the house every night of the week, there may be a problem with family cohesiveness. This type of situation could exist without trouble for a period of a month or so from time to time.

The eighteen-year-old should also have restrictions on coming and going. Even though legally an adult, the eighteen-year-old's maturity has increased by only one-seventeenth over the seventeen-year-old who is not an adult. At eighteen, a child requires and will often "ask for" restriction and some form of control from parents. Two nights per week until 1:00 A.M. and five nights per week until 11:30 P.M. should be sufficient for the eighteen-year-old. While this permits the "adult" to maintain some control on the new-found legal freedom, it also allows the "child" to continue to fit into the total family complex.

Friends

Parents have both the right and the obligation to know their child's friends, even those of the eighteen-year-old. This is sometimes difficult because children of this age are quite mobile and do not use the family house as a base for social activities. Nevertheless, it should be made clear to the sixteen-, seventeen-, and eighteen-year-old that parents' knowledge of their friends is important.

We believe that parents should express an aggressive interest in the friends of their eighteen-year-old daughters because pitfalls abound in our communities for the legally adult girl. We do not mean to imply that the boy who is eighteen cannot also fall in with the wrong crowd, but because an eighteen-year-old girl is more vulnerable, more adult supervision may be needed.

Dating/Curfew

Parents should express a high degree of interest in who their youngsters are dating, as well as in the date's family, values, and peer associations. We have often seen children doing very well until entering a dating relationship with a young adult from another background with significantly different values. Suddenly parents find their child split off from the family in terms of activities, thinking, and values. Caution should be exercised here.

Occasionally, a youngster in this age range is not dating and if this is the case, he or she should not be pushed. This is particularly true for the sixteen-year-old. If such a situation is present, the like sex parent could attempt to converse, gently, with much sensitivity, about the issue and learn what, if any, problems might be present. If a child is older than eighteen and still not socially interacting with the opposite sex, professional advice should perhaps be considered.

Occasionally, dating for youngsters in the sixteen to eighteen age range is excessive, and it becomes necessary for the parent to place restrictions on the number of dates a child has. This is fully appropriate and often advisable.

Dating should take place among youth of approximately the same age, regardless of sex. That is, seventeen-year-old boys should not date twelve-, thirteen-, or fourteen-year-old girls, or nineteen-, twenty-, and twenty-one-year-old women. Sixteen- and seventeen-year-old girls should be discouraged from dating men over twenty.

Sex

Sex relationships are all too frequently a part of dating at this age. Regardless of what others would have you believe, it is rare to find a young adult in this age who sufficiently understands the impact and complications of total sexual involvement. Sexual experimentation is in a far different category than consummation of the sex act, and consummation should have no place in the social activities of the sixteen-, seventeen-, and even eighteen-year-old.

It is at this age that questions concerning birth control often arise. The best method of birth control is to avoid sexual intercourse. Wise parents should strenuously encourage abstinence.

We have found that girls in this age range have a higher potential for difficulty than boys. Not only do girls tend to mature physically at a younger age, but female clothing styles have been introduced in recent years that are sexually revealing and provocative.

Fears and Irritability

For youth of this age, persistent, specific, and irrational fears should no longer be a problem. Intense fears, fears that interfere with life-style, obsessions, or compulsions should receive professional consultation.

The whining brought on by adolescence should have disappeared almost totally by age fifteen unless the youngster has been rather immature and is slow in development. Although parents of eleven-, twelve-, and thirteen-year-olds may disagree, if a youngster displays evidence of irritability, surliness, and poor communication during this age period, there tends to be fewer complications later in the child's life. The youngster is more manageable and controllable than if "adolescence" occurs at sixteen, seventeen, or eighteen.

Complaining and disagreeableness at this age may relate to poor recreational outlets or to boredom. Often, vocational difficulties occur in terms of finding meaningful employment after school, during summer vacation, or in place of school if the child is no longer in school.

Unhappiness with school is occasionally observed in this age range. Typically this dissatisfied individual is either in a poor school, has registered for a curriculum that is either too difficult or too easy, has been unfortunate in acquiring a group of poor teachers, or has been involved with the wrong peer group.

Romantic disappointments can certainly produce a high degree of irritability from ages fifteen to eighteen. However, depression associated with romantic breakups should not last longer than a month. If it does, parents should discuss the situation with the child and provide support, guidance and direct suggestions regarding activities to alleviate the depression.

No Spanking

As a general rule of thumb, *never spank* a teenager. This obviously would be treating him like a young child and most assuredly much resentment will result. If an aggressive physical contact by a parent occurs, there is the chance that the child may retaliate in kind. Reconciliation may be difficult.

Occasionally, a parent will persist in responding to a youngster of this age as if he or she were younger than the child's age dictates. Be aware that this age child is beginning to develop into adulthood. Parents should demonstrate their awareness of the child's growing maturity through such gestures as increased conversations with the child on a more adult level as well as giving greater responsibility. The teenager may show resentment at being dealt with as immature through such behavior as whining, criticizing younger siblings, overdependency, and general unhappiness. At this age it is increasingly important for parents to be aware of jealousies. Tensions can stem from the academic or athletic excellence of siblings or peers, vocational planning, peer acceptance, and physical attractiveness. Efforts should be made to ensure that the child is engaging in many experiences that are satisfying and ego building.

Allowance/Savings

The sixteen-, seventeen-, and eighteen-year-old should continue to receive allowance in addition to money earned through obligatory chores and responsibilities at home. The sixteen-year-old should receive a weekly allowance of $4, and the seventeen-year-old, a weekly allowance of $5. The eighteen-year-old should receive a weekly allowance of $6.

Weekly savings expected should be a minimum of sixty-five cents for the sixteen-year-old, seventy-five cents for the seventeen-year-old, and eighty-five cents for the eighteen-year-old. Of course, encouraging a child to save money may be a difficult task; however, parents and children should recognize that saving money is a characteristic that the wise, successful, and prudent adult must possess. Putting a youngster of this age in charge of a personal savings account at a bank is occasionally a successful motivator for saving.

When money is given as a gift, the sixteen-year-old may keep a maximum of $4, the seventeen-year-old $10 maximum, and the eighteen-year-old may keep all of the gift money. Between the allowance at this age and the work at home at ninety cents to $1 per hour, and perhaps a part-time job, the teenager should need little assistance for luxury or entertainment expenses. Of course, a child may need some help occasionally for large items.

Even if the family is wealthy, money should be dealt with in moderation with the child according to the rules outlined here. As any successful, wealthy parent realizes, a major factor in establishing and maintaining financial wealth is a healthy respect for money and its acquisition and expenditure. A child of this age should not be dealing in hundreds or thousands of dollars. Single dollars and tens of dollars are much more meaningful and appropriate. If there is success in managing small sums of money, the probability of the youngster successfully managing greater sums of money at an older age is increased.

Responsibilities

There are many people, including some "child experts," who believe that youngsters in this age range should not have responsibilities or rules in the home, because they are approaching adulthood and at the age of eighteen will legally become adults.

As with all child development, this age represents another gradual developmental change and nothing magical happens at the age of sixteen, seventeen, or eighteen. If a young person lives at home, he or she should share in the responsibilities as well as the privileges regardless of his age.

Actually, the entire issue of lack of responsibilities or adherence to rules has little to do with a child's age. Boarders in a hotel, for example, are required to abide by rules for orderly living regardless of their age. In fact, *more* rather than *fewer* commitments, responsibilities, and obligations are usually required for older people.

It seems rather senseless to teach a child that between the ages of sixteen and eighteen obligations and responsibilities in the home somehow become diluted or disappear. The sixteen-, seventeen-, and eighteen-year-old continues to need the security of structure and the unspoken message implicit in family and home responsibilities. This message should clearly state that the youngster still has a home, is still a part of the family, and that a contribution is both necessary and advisable.

Sixteen- to eighteen-year-olds should be expected to have three responsibilities per day without pay and in addition, work two hours per week at home for pay. The sixteen-year-old should be paid ninety cents an hour for work in the home, the seventeen- and eighteen-year-old should be paid approximately $1 per hour. If a child of this age has a regular job, even though part time, the work time at home can be reduced or eliminated because that is mainly designed to give the child some work to do and additional income. Responsibilities in the home on a daily basis should not be eliminated.

The suggestions in Table 14 for housework may be used as regular responsibilities for no pay or as additional sources of income for the child.

Table 14.   Ages Sixteen through Eighteen

Job	Salary*
Shovel snow	$1.50
Wash car (outside)	2.50
Clean car (inside)	1.00
Clean garage or basement (sweeping, hosing, throw away junk)	1.50
Give dog a bath	.35
Pull weeds (one large lawn bag)	1.50
Fertilize lawn	2.00
Mow lawn	3.50
Trim grass	1.50
Trim hedges	3.00
Rake leaves and pine needles	1.25
Vacuum and sweep house	1.25
Clean bathroom floors	1.00 each
Clean kitchen floor	1.00
Clean windows and sliding glass doors	.30 each
Wash screens	.30 each
Polish silver or polish furniture	1.25
Go to store and do shopping	1.50
Wash dishes and/or load dishwasher	.50
Babysit younger children	.60 per hour
Painting	1.50 per hour
Change car oil	1.50

*Average of $1.50 per hour

Behavior Contract

For problem behaviors in this age group, we have seen success from parents entering into a "contract" with their child. A legal-looking document, with dates, signatures, and specific statement of agreement, is transacted between parents and child. The child agrees to a certain specific set of behaviors, and the parent agrees to a specific set of rewards for the accomplishment of the behavior.

Driving

Sixteen-, seventeen-, and eighteen-year-olds should be encouraged to learn how to drive as soon as possible because this skill will help them relate more closely with friends and participate more in community and school functions. Parents should participate in teaching their children to drive even if the children receive driver education in school or take private driving lessons. We find that this gives parents an opportunity to teach from their own experience. It also shows the children that parents have an interest in the development of a skill that the children see as positive, giving them independence and responsibility. In this way, parents can associate themselves with some of the real privileges that children earn as they move along. This also helps bring another activity back into the home rather than splitting it off and having the child taught entirely by outsiders.

It has become quite common to find sixteen- and seventeen-year-olds driving to other parts of the state or even across the country with other teenagers. Unless proper chaperoning takes place, or the child is extremely responsible and mature, trips of this nature invite trouble. If such a trip is requested, the presence of a mature adult as chaperone is highly advisable.

Employment

Employment for the youngster in this age range as busboy or waitress is available. But if a youngster is employed, parents would be wise to be certain that there is not an excessive amount of fatigue or that commitments at home and school are suffering.

Parents should also be alert to the fact that occasionally an employer will thrust a youngster of this age range into positions of responsibility that are difficult to manage and can cause undue anxiety and stress. Conversely, many menial jobs available for youth in this age range are extremely boring and tedious for the intelligent and creative youngster, and restlessness or failure on the job may occur.

Typically, confusion might occur at this age as to whether the child is to attend college or enter directly into employment or vocational training. If this type of confusion persists until a person is nineteen or twenty years old, a vocational evaluation should be sought from a competent professional.

Drinking

The issue of a child drinking, either within or outside of the home, frequently arises. In our experience, we have found that it may be wise for parents to occasionally offer the sixteen-, seventeen-, or eighteen-year-old a small amount of beer or wine with meals. This may serve to take some of the glow, excitement, and the forbidden aspects out of drinking. It can serve to teach the young adult how to drink in moderation, and he or she can learn how drinking can complement food and social gatherings without being abused.

Enjoy!

In regard to the issue of drinking (but certainly in many other areas as well) parents too frequently become associated with the restraints on their children's behavior. They do not associate themselves with some of the luxuries and privileges that their children enjoy and that they can enjoy with them. After all, it is parents who have done the majority of the work. Parents have brought the children along to a certain level, and they should have the privilege of enjoying their child's maturity also. This pleasure need not occur entirely outside of the home with strangers.

High School

If children have had academic success in earlier grades and demonstrate maturity, they can probably make their way through a public high school without major damage to their values or motivation. Parents are advised to take a close look at their children's courses and books and to be wary of new and experimental programs. This is especially important if these programs have a heavy weighting of weak academic students or students with behavior problems.

Large unscheduled gaps of time and split sessions are not generally recommended. Parents should inquire into the realities and practicalities of that new system if your child is involved.

Incredible as it may seem, some public and even private high schools are introducing new programs wholesale, without local research and pilot studies. These programs are sometimes thoroughly enjoyed by the students. When achievement falls and parents complain, they are told that these new programs cannot be accurately evaluated by traditional achievement techniques! Parents should remember that a child's enjoyment of school is not the only or even most important criterion of the school's success.

College Ahead?

If a child is planning on college, he had better be achieving above average on school achievement tests comparing him with *national*—not local—norms. Students planning on college should discuss the requirements thoroughly with an appropriate school guidance counselor early in their freshman year.

Don't Quit!

One additional note seems extremely appropriate in discussing this age range. We find that many conscientious parents perform their parenting jobs extremely well and raise sound, contributing young adult citizens. But then they quit after the child graduates from high school. If the child is to attend a college or university, Don't Quit the Parenting Role Yet!

Parents should not turn their children over to a university or college that can undo or erode what the parents and the children have so diligently nurtured. Many universities are concerned with exposing students to new ideas and "alternative life-styles." These include open coeducational dorms, a neglect of religious values, and a cynicism concerning society's institutions, including law, government, and the family. The "do your own (selfish) thing" way of thinking can become a way of existence.

The number of college freshmen, sophomores, and juniors that the authors have seen professionally, who are confused and bewildered about the values taught in these types of universities, is frighteningly large. This type of confusion has also come to our attention when young college graduates attempt to apply the values and approaches taught at these universities. Much to their regret and surprise, they are failures back in the "real world."

Parents should have the courage to scrutinize the college that their graduating high school child has chosen in the same fashion that the child's grade school had been scrutinized. Is the philosophy of the college consistent with the philosophy that has guided your home? Are the regulations, codes of conduct, and student restrictions proper for the child and extensions of what the parent believes is correct? Do not be impressed or overwhelmed by "big-name schools" or universities with strong academic reputations. Investigate! Life at universities has changed considerably during the past five to fifteen years, and the school that enjoyed a superior reputation twenty years ago may not be the school for everyone.

We recognize that parents cannot shelter their loved ones forever. However, it is through selective sheltering of the child that values and successful life-styles can be taught.

The longer parents and children can maintain the relationships described in this book, the more successful will be the children's transition into happy adulthood. The twenty-year-old is in a better position to make proper judgments about values and life-styles than the eighteen-year-old, and the twenty-five-year-old engages in this task more successfully than the twenty-year-old, and so on.

Unlike some humanists and "generation gap" proponents, the authors believe that parents may continue to influence their children even into adulthood. (See Figure 7.) The authors continue to seek the wisdom and advice of their own parents in many areas of their own lives.

Figure 7. Parent Versus Child Self-Direction

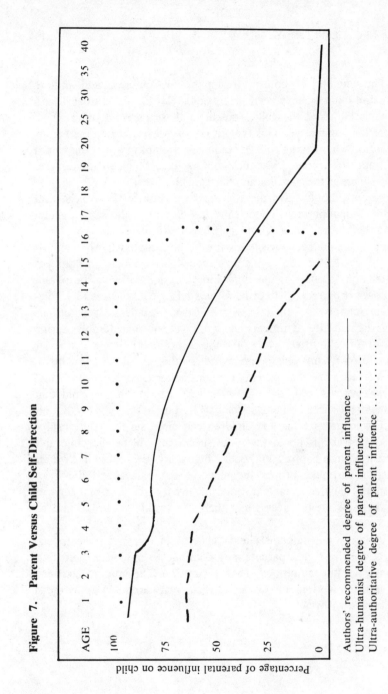

Authors' recommended degree of parent influence ——————
Ultra-humanist degree of parent influence - - - - - - - - -
Ultra-authoritative degree of parent influence ············

11 Myths of Child-Rearing

1. *When discipline works, it should work immediately.*

We know that learning does not take place in this way. A child may often test a parent or try to make the problem worse immediately after a reasonable and potentially workable discipline is introduced. Parents must be consistent with discipline and keep track over a period of days or weeks to see if the discipline is effective. Do not discard a discipline approach too rapidly or hold to unreasonable expectations for immediate results.

2. *If a specific discipline works, you will know by the child's reactions.*

On the contrary, when a parent introduces an effective method of discipline, children may retort that it does not bother them. A child might say: "I would just as soon be sitting in my room as outside playing." It is unfortunate when parents believe this reasoning. Do not expect children to verbally admit that parental discipline is effective.

3. *Parents should never lose their tempers.*

Parents will lose their tempers on occasion. They are human and should show their children that they can regain control after a loss of temper.

217

4. *In order to be fair, each child in a family should be treated in exactly the same way.*

This falsehood can be detrimental to children. Children must realize that responsibilities and privileges go together, and that older siblings have both more responsibilities and more privileges. Throughout life, rewards are not received equally by everyone. A brother should not receive a present simply because a sister is having a birthday and parents believe he will feel left out or resentful if he does not receive a present.

Conditions in this world are not always fair and certainly they are not equal. Trying to treat all children in a family equally may be based on one of the "great American myths": that all people are to receive equal treatment regardless of the circumstances.

5. *You should always reason things out with children.*

This is certainly not always the case. In some situations, and at some age levels, it is appropriate to attempt to reason things out. At other times it can be inappropriate. The reader is referred to Chapter 6 through 10.

6. *All you need to raise children is good communications.*

Communication is a "wastebasket" term that is much too broad. It is similar to the terms "immaturity" and "lazy" in its vagueness. Even families in trouble are able to communicate; however, they disagree about the *content* of their communications.

7. *Out of the mouths of babes . . .*

If brilliant statements made by children did not represent the exception, we would not make such a fuss about these statements when they occur. Children lack the judgment, experience, and intellectual capacity of adults and, therefore, are usually ineffective in making decisions when compared to adults.

8. *Children are more sensitive and more capable of feeling than adults. They are more aware of other people's feelings and can immediately sense whether an adult is a sincere or insincere person.*

This is nonsense. Adults can easily fool children and often do so. While children have the capacity to feel deeply, they do not have the empathy that most adults possess. For example, recall the cruel and often unthinking remarks children make about other children. This occurs with young children because the self-concept is not highly developed until after the age of ten or eleven. Children cannot empathize with others until they have an awareness of their own selves.

9. *Parents and children should share the same interests.*

How can grown adults possibly enjoy putting a three or four piece puzzle together? They may enjoy watching a child's efforts at mastery but are rarely interested in the activity itself. Often this is the reason that parents, especially fathers, do not spend time with their younger children.

Parents sometimes believe they must find some shared activity and spend long periods of time participating in this activity with their child. It is much preferable for them to spend smaller amounts of time, even fifteen minute intervals a few times a week, doing something the child prefers to do. Parents may admit to themselves that this may not be the most exciting activity, but they should persist with it for the fifteen minutes.

This is much better than parents finding some activity that they enjoy but that their child does not. For example, fishing with a younger child who is active and easily bored will often result in anger for both parent and child.

The quality of individual time spent with a child is often more important than the quantity. However, parents must always be available if their child runs into difficulty and needs them. They should not use any rationalization to justify spending little time with the family or a particular child.

10. *The way to get through to adolescents is to dress like them, talk like them, and listen to popular music.*

If this were true, imagine what parents would be required to do in order to get through to a two-year-old. Nothing will lose the respect of an adolescent more quickly than a forty-two-year-old "teeny bopper."

Most middle-class adolescents do not live in a secretive and separate subculture. Children will probably always have their fads in dress, music, and a few special words that can hardly be described as an extensive subculture vocabulary. Remember, these interests are not developed by the child but rather by adults who are selling a product or a philosophy.

11. *Children are intricate, complex, fragile, and should not experience frustration.*

All humans are intricate and complex, but children can hardly be considered fragile. That most children have survived many conflicting "child development" theories is a tribute to their stability.

It is certainly a myth that children must never be frustrated. How else will they learn to tolerate frustration?

12. *Teacher knows best.*

This is true when teacher *does* know best. Most teachers are conscientious and competent. The teacher is usually correct when there is a teacher-student conflict regarding homework or the teaching of basic skills such as reading, spelling, and arithmetic. Teachers are human, however. There are good teachers and bad teachers, troubled teachers and fatigued teachers.

In recent years, some teachers have been required to instruct in values as well as basic academic skills in order to help develop the "whole child." While the teacher's intent may be worthwhile, necessary skills and sophistication are often lacking. Also, the values taught may be in conflict with those of the child's home.

13. *You should never help your children with their studies.*

This is true if the children do not need help with their studies. If a child comes to a parent for help with homework, parents should provide help and encouragement as long as they do not do the work for the child. A child's request for help should not be used as an opportunity to spend long hours teaching the child.

14. *Children who don't do well in school are lazy.*

If this were true, then why does the same child work so hard in nonacademic areas? Children are naturally curious. If they appear lazy in school they may be in the wrong school, the wrong class, have a learning disability, have experienced poor teaching in the past, or show habitual patterns of failure that block their natural curiosity.

15. *Most adolescents and young adults are rebellious and want to revolutionize their country and system of government.*

Check the youth vote in local and national elections and you may be surprised. Adolescence is a normal time for questioning institutions and values, but most of the middle-class youth of today are rather conservative in their outlook. Once again, adults with vested interests have a tendency to generalize the extreme behavior of a minority to the majority. Remember that adolescents are more open in discussing such areas as sex and drugs. Do not be stampeded by crisis-seekers into scrutiny and watchfulness. This will communicate a lack of trust to a child, especially when the child knows there is no reason to doubt.

16. *If parents do an excellent job of child-rearing, their children will not have problems no matter how bad the peer group or school.*

Peer group and school influence are major factors. A negative influence from peers and school can certainly undo the excellent efforts of parents. Interestingly, it is also true that if the school and peer group are excellent, the child is not likely to have problems, even if the parents carry out their job poorly.

17. *Children should not be given an allowance because they just squander money.*

It is by squandering that a child may learn how to save money and be responsible for budgeting.

18. *If children are placed under parental rules and regulations, they will not be free.*

The railroad boxcar is free to move only as it is confined to the railroad track. When placed in a pasture, free of its track, it has no freedom of movement whatsoever.

19. *The family is a democracy.*

This is true only if everyone in the family is eighteen years of age or older and self-supporting.

20. *Families should eat their meals together no matter what!*
Nothing is true "no matter what." Dinner time can often be a good time for family communication and togetherness. However, this may not be true, especially when the children are young. If dinner time becomes stressful and adds turmoil to the family, alternative plans should be considered. Parents might eat separately from the children for several evening meals during the week. There is nothing sacred about family dinner.

21. *Children go through stages of "bad" behavior or slowed development, and there really isn't much to worry about.*
True, but it depends upon how *long* the stages last and how serious the problems are.

22. *A child should never repeat a grade in school because he or she will feel like a faliure.*
If a grade is repeated children can feel failure, although they sometimes feel relief. On the other hand, if youngsters need to repeat a grade and do not, they will feel much more like failures as they cope with the frustration of competing with children who are more advanced.

It is important to remember that if a child has a learning disability or has not learned the basics in school, merely holding the child back probably will not help in the long run. It will give the child an extra year to mature, but if he or she has a learning disability, specialized remedial tutoring or other help in addition to being held back will be required.

23. *A child should never skip a grade in school because he or she will be too young for his or her peers and have social problems in high school.*
If a child needs to be advanced because of high intelligence and general maturity, this may be the only solution possible.

Some schools now offer special programs for gifted children that place a child with other bright children for a portion of the school day. Such programs may help but much depends upon *who* teaches them and what *values* are taught. While these programs can allow an exchange of ideas and an association with children of equal intelligence, we have seen other problems arise. A child is returned to regular class for most of the school day, and we have seen children become even more frustrated, troublesome, and bored than before they entered a program for the "gifted."

24. *A child needs to face up to problems and learn not to run away from them.*

In life, learning how to "run away" from harmful situations is a desirable, maturing experience. If a child is in a bad situation, whether it be in the school, the community center or the peer group, parents should consider removing the child from that situation as soon as possible. In the "good old bad old days," the parent was usually correct in making a child face up to an environment, because the environment was a constant factor, and well known by the parent. In more recent times, the community has undergone rapid changes. Parents should be vigilant of changing values, just as they should remain aware of developmental changes within their children.

25. *All schools are the same.*

There are great differences within and among schools. Schools are very important in molding the personality of the child and can be an overriding influence on the child's development.

Schools differ in their approaches to academics and the importance they place upon basic skills such as reading. They also vary considerably in the values they attempt to teach. Religious and many secular private schools teach a clear set of values toward work and life. Many public schools and state universities attempt to teach "critical thinking" rather than "values" per se but in reality are teaching values nonetheless.

26. *Parents really know very little about their own children.*

No one really knows more about a child than the parents. Parents are human and have their blind spots. They may be too close to their children to analyze them objectively. We have seen parents accused of not knowing their children because they do not know the proper words to describe feelings and emotions. But it has been rare for us to see parents who are not knowledgeable about their own children.

27. *I cannot ask my child to pick up clothes and toys because my wife and I do not pick up after ourselves.*

You had better try. You are probably required to be organized in your job and the home is your child's major area of responsibility if he or she is below the age of thirteen. Children need to learn organization and respect for property.

28. *I would like to be positive with my children but they do absolutely nothing that is worthy of praise.*

They probably do several hundred things each day but you are taking them for granted. If the children walk from the front door to the kitchen without stumbling and breaking a piece of furniture, perhaps you should count that behavior as a positive one.

29. *I will not bribe my child to work around the house.*

Your child should be required to do some work without any type of reward, social or material. But for work over and above that required as a contribution to the family, the child should be rewarded. If you believe that is a bribe, then refuse to accept your next paycheck.

30. *Behavior charts are for babies, and they don't work.*

Charts are used in the military, and charts are used in high level business management. If a child's behavior chart does not work as a temporary catalyst, it is because the parents have unreasonable responsibilities on the chart or unreasonable consequences or rewards.

31. *Some parents allow children to develop on their own and teach that values outside a person do not exist.*

You are *always* teaching a value, even while denying that guidelines exist.

32. *Behaviorists do not teach values; they deal strictly with behavior and not with the core of the individual.*

You always teach a value whether or not you are a behaviorist.

12 When to Go for Help and Where

Determining when a child needs professional help is not as difficult as one might think. There are two fairly simple rules of thumb to follow here: First, when a child is chronically unhappy for several months, parents should consider outside help. If parents have tried the suggestions outlined throughout this book and the child's misery continues, outside professional assistance should be sought.

A second indication of the need for outside help is when a child is receiving a great deal of pressure from siblings, peers, community (school or teacher, for example), or from parents. It is absolutely no help to a child to conclude that "He is just lazy in school and will have to straighten up" or that "She must learn the hard way" to get along with others.

Looking for someone to help a child is also not as difficult as one might think. The child should be taken to someone the parents respect and who has knowledge of the child. This can be a pediatrician or family doctor, a minister, rabbi, or priest, teacher or counselor. Often trusted friends can help here also. This respected person should not simply supply a professional category such as "psychologist" or "psychiatrist" as a resource, but rather should give the parents the *name* of someone he or she knows that has been successful with the *type* of problem the child presents. The professional should have the proper credentials as well as a reputation for successful work.

Parents should avoid turning to the Yellow Pages or taking a child to a clinic where the parent will not have a choice of the professional person who will work with the child. Do not rely on advertising for clinical or educational services. Do not rely on fads.

If parents know someone whose child was helped by a certain person, program, or school, they should check this out with a pediatrician or another trusted professional. Two children may appear to have the same type of problem, when, in fact, they are quite different.

A few special cautions are in order here. When professional mental health assistance is called for, parents should make every effort to have the child seen by a licensed psychologist, board certified psychiatrist, or social worker. There are many public agencies, organizations, and programs that purport to provide psychological counseling, psychotherapy, and other services offered by psychologists, psychiatrists, and social workers. Unfortunately, many of these organizations are permitted by law to certify their own employees, and they can award them the title of "psychologist" or "social worker" even though these people do not have the proper education, credentials, or background. Many of them could not be licensed by a state board of examiners and permitted to practice privately.

We have seen much heartache and difficulty resulting from attempts by unqualified people to provide psychological or counseling services. One of the most commonly seen errors, and this can happen easily, is for the individuals to establish a relationship with a child that neglects parental needs and results in a separation of the child from the family. These advisors may have a strong need to develop a relationship with the child and a strong bias toward believing that parents are at the root of all children's problems. This person may not communicate sufficiently with the parents and may not even learn the facts of the situation. Parents frequently then feel guilty about their parenting ability; they feel disillusioned, and the problem often becomes more complicated. The overall result is that the parent often gives up on professional consultation, and the child may not receive the needed help.

Parents have the right to discuss the credentials, education, and certification or licensing of any professional person from whom they seek assistance. Goals of any proposed treatment are legitimate topics of discussion, and parents have the right to review the direction of treatment with the provider of services at any time. Parents should not be dismayed if they are criticized for expressing an interest in the credentials of the helper and the nature of treatment. They should not be deterred or confused by tedious jargon or the implication that they are impertinent or not "with it" for asking questions about what will happen to the child. Parents should not blindly entrust their child's life to a stranger with a title.

Schools are educational organizations. A classroom teacher should no more be permitted to diagnose the nature of a behavior problem than to diagnose the nature of an abdominal pain. Effective psychological treatment can rarely be performed by school personnel.

The institutional structure of the school often prevents a professional approach even in those situations where the consultant is competent and well trained. School personnel may be participating in a training program that has time limits, and corrective help may be broken off abruptly. Many school programs close in the summer, and the child is allowed to regress. School personnel may not be able legally to provide help outside the school building and usually cannot be reached at home in crisis situations. These limitations result because schools were not established to provide in-depth, around-the-clock, and fully responsible psychological services to children.

If a recommendation is made for a child to see a specific psychologist, counselor, or social worker, parents should feel free to investigate the nature of this individual's credentials and education. You probably choose an attorney rather cautiously to assist you with a simple legal issue. You probably also choose a T.V. repairman with caution. Certainly, you should exercise considerably more care when choosing someone to help with your child's life.

We believe that parents love their children and want the very best for them. Remember, decisions made at these times are critical and could determine the direction of your child's life as well as your own.

Bibliography

Cain, Arthur. *Young People and Sex.* New York: John Day, 1967.

Developmental Checklist. Mack R. Hicks, Ph.D. NCS/Interpretive Scoring Systems, 4401 West 76th St., Minneapolis, Minn. 55435 (1979).

Dobson, James C. *Dare to Discipline.* Wheaton, Ill.: Tyndale House, 1972.

Gardner, Richard A. *Minimal Brain Dysfunction.* New York: Jason Aronson, 1973.

Gardner, Richard A. *The Boys and Girls Book about Divorce.* New York. Bantam, 1970.

Ginot, Haim. *Between Parent and Child.* New York: Macmillan, 1965.

Goff, Beth. *Where Is Daddy? The Story of a Divorce.* Boston: Bekin Press, 1969.

Lindley, O. R. "An Experiment with Parents Handling Behavior at Home." *Johnstone Bulletin* (1966), 9:27-36.

McGuide, Mebelle B. *Finger and Action Rhymes.* New York: F. A. Owen, 1970.

National Commission on the Reform of Secondary Education. *A Report to the Public and the Profession.* New York: McGraw-Hill, 1973.

Public Broadcasting System. The Advocates: Fight of the Week. *Should the Law Allow Birth Control Treatment for Teenagers Without Parents' Consent?* May 8, 1973.

Thompson, Lloyd J. "Learning Disabilities: An Overview." *American Journal of Psychiatry* (April 1973), 130, no. 4: 393-99.

Venereal Disease Statistics. *1973 National Report.* Personal Communication. County Health Department, St. Petersburg, Florida.

Zigler, Edward. "I am Growing Up, Learning and Loving." *Human Behavior* (March 1973), 2:65-67.

Index

231